Nadia describes herself as being "the happiest person I know" and has made it her life's mission as a life coach and author to help millions of people across the globe by igniting their inner light and creating their own version of an abundantly happy life. After a near-death experience in her twenties, Nadia gave up her successful business in the UK to live her dream life in Italy and has been living there ever since. The great loves of her life are her two children, summer days on the beach with her family, the well-being of herself and others, and writing her books.

My Growing Heart is dedicated to...

My two beautiful children, Leon and Maia. My love for them and my desire for them to live happy, peaceful and joyful lives inspired me to write this book. They are, and always will be, a part of my soul. Leon and Maia, this book is for you. To be a guide and light to help you to navigate yourselves through life with ease and grace. To know that at any age and stage you can turn to me for guidance and love. My love for you is immeasurable and I am filled with gratitude to have been given the honour to bring your beautiful souls into this world.

To my wonderful late parents, Franco Cheung Yau Wong and Maria Teresa Wong (nee Ciardiello), for all that they gave me in life, and in death. For teaching me by example and for not giving me everything that I wanted.

To Gaetano, my husband and lifetime growth buddy. For listening to me day in and day out for 25 years (no easy feat), for sharing your life with me and for making a beautiful family with me. I am truly grateful for the incredible life that we have created together, built with our love.

To my nephew, Natalino De Martino, for his help in getting my manuscript into digital form and keeping me right with all the techy stuff which made my life so much easier. You mean more to me than you will ever know.

To the beautiful Genesis Angela Gobbo for reminding me what it feels like to be a teenager and for your support and encouragement while writing this book.

To Graeme Leavy for being such a big part of my life as we transitioned into adulthood together. You will always be a part of the Wong family.

To all my amazing friends, old and new. There are too many of you to name but you know who you are.

To the late Judith Scott. For her heartfelt poem that fuelled me and pushed me forward when I needed a reminder of the importance of my work. And to her mum, my friend, Joyce Syme, for allowing me to share Judith's precious words.

To those of you that have ever hurt me, thank you for the experiences that pushed me to learn and grow from, to enable me to become a better human being. We all make mistakes in life and I forgive you. Without you and the emotional pain

I suffered, I would not be the strong and courageous woman I am today. I genuinely thank you from the bottom of my heart.

To all those that believed in me and my work and have supported me on this journey. I am truly grateful for your encouragement and love.

Finally, I would like to thank my wonderful friend, coach and mentor, Heather Gordon, for her unwavering support and love. For seeing my potential even before I did. This book exists because you do. Without you, this book would have remained a seed in my heart and mind, but your loving light and presence in my life allowed my seed to grow into my dream.

Wishing you all a lifetime of happiness, health and love.
With all my love,

Nadia
xxx

Nadia Wong

MY GROWING HEART

AUSTIN MACAULEY PUBLISHERS™

LONDON • CAMBRIDGE • NEW YORK • SHARJAH

A CIP catalogue record for this title is available from the British Library.

ISBN 9781528946476 (Paperback)
ISBN 9781528971782 (ePub e-book)

www.austinmacauley.com

First Published (2021)
Austin Macauley Publishers Ltd
25 Canada Square
Canary Wharf
London
E14 5LQ

My thanks go out to everyone that I have ever loved for making my heart grow to the size it has. Especially my beautiful sisters, Marisa and Gisella, for being the wonderful and loving human beings that you are. And to all my family. I love you all with all my heart.

Introduction

This is the part of the book that gives me a chance to make a good first impression, for you to decide to read this book instead of muttering *"Boring..."* under your breath, tossing it to one side. If you are reluctant to read, I hear you, because I *was* you. You may find this hard to believe but up until the age of 20, I'd only read about 5 books...and I only read them because I was forced to, so I get where you are coming from. You may be a different kind of person than I was at your age, but the last thing I wanted to do in my spare time was read. Nevertheless, here I am many years later writing books... Who would've known?

So why *do* I write? Because I have so many life and love lessons to teach that are bursting to come out of me, to help you on your journey through life. I needed this book when I was your age, but because I didn't have it, I decided to create something that would've made my life so much easier... To save *you* a lot of unnecessary heartache. Think of me as your fairy godmother, here to be your guide, to help you become the shining light that you were born to be, to steer you in the right direction. I learned many life lessons the hard way, and you will learn some that way too, but there are so many mistakes I could've avoided if I'd known what I know now or if I had a fairy godmother in my life. Essentially, I've become a person that I wish I'd had to hold my hand, not just as I transitioned into adulthood, but throughout my life. You may think that as you grow older, you will naturally grow wiser, but that is not necessarily true. Wisdom doesn't just happen, we need to seek out the truth about life for ourselves and take our own path, not simply follow the path that we think we *should* take or follow the crowd. It's about creating a life that makes *us* happy, regardless of what others think or say. I am here to help you to know your true self, love your true self and to trust your true self by listening to your own intuition and decide who you want to *be* in life and what you want to do. I'm not here to tell you what to be and do but to ask you the right questions. I don't have the answers for you to live a happy, successful life full of love, light and joy. *You* do! Everything any of us need in life is already within us. We simply need to look within ourselves to find it. This book is a journey, a process of understanding your growing heart, your growing mind and your growing soul.

Life can seem complicated if we see it as complicated, but if we see it for the beauty that it really is and through following some simple but profound guidelines, it can and will be truly beautiful.

You may be wondering who I am and what qualifies me to write this book. First of all, I've been where you are now and I not only survived, I thrived. I'm also a life coach and teach people of all ages how to live life with more joy. Being a mother to a 15-year-old boy and a 12-year-old girl is also a daily reminder of the challenges of a growing heart, discovering who you are and who you want to become. You are growing up so fast and it's not always easy trying to keep up with all the emotions and physical changes that are taking place right now. Believe me when I say that it's not easy for us as parents either. We are all taking this unknown journey together but we get to choose whether to grow together or grow apart. I only have one real regret in my life and that is the way I treated my mum when I was growing up. Now that she is no longer in my life, I wish I could go back and give her a hug and tell her how much I love her and appreciate her. She was not a perfect mother but neither am I. I simply know that I am doing my best, and so was she.

My Growing Heart is designed to help you to understand who you are and allow your true self to shine through. Each and every one of us were born into this world as pure and perfect souls, untainted by life, but it's up to us how we choose to live our lives. We can choose to be happy, loving, kind and honest souls and live life to the full or we can equally choose to be unhappy, unkind and selfish. The choice is entirely ours but first we have to decide what kind of person we want to be and what kind of life we want to live.

A lot of adults live their whole lives not knowing who they are and spend their lives unhappily searching for that missing piece and never find it because they failed to look inside themselves. They looked for external factors to make them feel complete but we are each whole and complete beings, and no thing, activity or person can fill that void except ourselves.

The sooner you learn who you are and who you want to become, the better your life will be. You don't need to have all the answers to life's questions right now, as it is a continual journey through life as you grow, but when you know who and what you are looking for in life, you will find them with more ease.

You have the whole world in your hands and it's up to you if you play the game of life. You can choose whether to take hold of the control panel and play your life with passion or you can sit back and watch others take the controls and play your life for you. It is entirely up to you.

Parents, grandparents and those that love you can help you navigate through the game of life, to enable you to know where the dangers are as they have been playing this game for quite some time and know how it works. However, they are not perfect either and will make mistakes, as we all do. One thing to remember, though, is that they are on your team, and they want you to win with outstanding scores.

Welcome to the game of life… Now let's play!

Love Lesson #1
Who Am I?

"Always be yourself because an original is always better than a copy."

The first step on the journey through life is to understand who we are and to realise that every single one of us are pure love and of great worth, even though we are all so very different. We all come in different shapes, sizes and colours but we are all of *equal* worth. What sets us apart and makes us extraordinary is not how we look or what gifts and talents we have but how we choose to behave and how we treat other people.

We have one life and one chance to be our very best. We were each born at the right time and have a purpose for being here right now. We may never know exactly why we were born at this time but we have to trust in the plan of the universe and know that we were just meant to be. By our small acts of love and kindness we can transform lives and hearts just by being ourselves. We don't need to have powerful positions to play a valuable part in life, all we have to do is be our best selves by spreading love and lifting others up.

Some of us were born to be teachers and influencers, some to be leaders, some to be light workers, here to lift and inspire others, bringing more love and light to the world, but we must remember that we all have a purpose and we all matter.

I know I was born to do exactly what I am doing now. I was born to awaken the awareness in my fellow beings to help them to know themselves, to love themselves, to realise their worth and live purpose filled lives. We don't always know why we are here or what our purpose is but every step forward we take will lead us to where we need to be. We can make a huge difference to many lives even without realising it, simply by showing up as the best versions of ourselves.

It could be a simple act of kindness that could transform the life of another. Even just a smile can brighten someone's day. We all have the power to make others smile regardless of who we are, so let's not waste it.

Let's begin this book with a little experiment to open your mind to the power you have over the simple things in life.

Find a mirror or put your phone on selfie mode and look at yourself. Even if you don't feel happy at the moment, put the biggest, cheesiest smile on your face and keep it there for at least five seconds. Apart from feeling slightly silly, how else do you feel?

You can stop smiling now, but you'll find that it won't be easy as you are now smiling for real. Did you feel the difference? Smiling makes us feel happier and lighter even if we feel we have nothing much to smile about. We don't need to be happy to smile but if we smile, we will feel happier. When we smile at others, it not only brightens their day, as it forces them to smile back, it brightens our own. If we say we can't smile, it's because we are choosing not to smile. If we are able bodied and we are told to lift up our arms we can do it no matter how we feel so we can smile no matter how we feel. One thing that we must always remember is that we each have the power to lift others up by simply smiling. We cannot make others happy, as each of us are responsible for our own happiness, but we *can* make them smile!

By answering the following questions as openly and honestly as you possibly can, you will start to know who you are, who you want to be, and what you truly want in life. There are no right or wrong answers as there is only one you. We want others to love and value us for who we truly are but how can they know who we are if we don't know ourselves? Let's take this journey together, one love lesson at a time.

Knowing Myself

1. On a scale of 1–10, how well do I know myself? (1 being I don't know who I am or what I want from life, 10 being I know exactly who I am and what I want to do with my life)

2. What are my five best qualities as a human being, and why?
    For example.

    a) I'm a loving human being. I feel love for all people and it breaks my heart to see anyone suffer unnecessarily.
    b) I'm playful and love being silly and to make others laugh.
    c) I'm hard working but also love to have fun while doing so.

    a.
    b.
    c.
    d.
    e.

3. What are my top three gifts and talents? For example.

    a) I have the ability to see the beauty and potential in most people even if they don't see it themselves.

    b) I'm creative and good at making things and creating recipes for healthy foods.

    a.

    b.

    c.

4. What three things am I most passionate about? (What do I love doing that I get really excited about?)

    For example. Helping others, running, cooking.

    a.

    b.

    c.

5. What (not who) makes me happy?

    For example. Being on the beach with my family and playing in the sea, being cuddled up with my family on the couch watching a funny movie in our PJs.

6. What kind of person do I want to be in life?

    For example. I want to be a good person and be a good example to my children. I want to make a difference in the lives of others by helping them find peace in mind, body and spirit.

    Now it is your turn:

    I want to be…

7. If I could be anything I choose to be in life, what would I be and do?

8. Why do I want this? How would it benefit me?

9. How much control do I believe I have over my life, my happiness and my destiny?

10. How much control would I like to have over my life, my happiness and my destiny?

11. What is good in my life at the moment?

12. What needs to improve in my life?

The most important lesson that I have learned in my life is that no one else is responsible for our happiness. No matter who we are or what we have been through, we are each responsible for ourselves and our emotions. Happiness is a choice and a state of mind and no one else, no matter how much we love them, has the capability to make us happy. They can make us smile and make us feel good being around them but we can't be happy *for* them and vice versa.

The second most important lesson I have learned in life is that we are at our happiest when we are serving our life's purpose and serving others, which I will talk about a little later.

The sooner we understand that we have control of our lives and that we are in the driving seat of our lives, the sooner we can be free to be who we want to be and go where we want to go.

We can choose to be the driver of our own lives and go where we want to go, or we can be a passenger in other people's lives.

My Guiding Principles

Our guiding principles are a list of our core values that we choose to live by that become part of us as we go through life becoming better every day. It's like having our own personal rulebook that we have written for ourselves to remind us who we are and why we are here.

We were all born into this world as perfect and flawless souls that are instinctively good and loving beings but sometimes life can lead us astray as we try to fit in and be 'normal'.

"Well, everyone else does it so it must be okay!" is what we tell ourselves, but if we don't make a conscious decision to be true to who *we* are, we can get lost in the fog and find it hard to find ourselves later on.

When we live by our guiding principles, we can live in peace with ourselves, knowing that we are being and doing our very best.

Our guiding principles are a list of standards that we choose to live by in order to be happy with ourselves and to know we are of worth. If we live our lives according to our guiding principles then we feel good and happy, but if we go against them, we feel bad and question who we really are. Writing our own list helps us to stay on track so we are able to make better choices, make less mistakes and therefore avoid that horrible guilty feeling of wishing we had behaved differently.

For example, if you are with a group of friends and they start laughing at and teasing someone that has a disability or is singled out for some reason (even just for a laugh), what do you do?

You could do a number of things. You could choose to:

- Join in and laugh so you don't look out of place with your friends.
- Stay silent.
- Walk away having nothing to do with it.
- Stand up for the victim and be brave enough to say, "That's just not funny and that is out of order."
- Go up to the victim and say, "Just ignore them. They think they are being funny but they are not."

If you already have a list of your guiding principles fixed in your heart and mind, and know what kind of person you are or want to be, you will find it easier to react to these kinds of situations and make the right choice. If being kind to everyone is on your list you will not accept what is going on and do something about it. Alternatively, if you are unsure of who you are and you have not made a commitment to being kind to everyone, you may even join in and laugh with them without even thinking about it, but if that person runs away crying you may feel very differently and feel horrible about yourself after.

We have to ask ourselves, "If I was in this same situation but on the receiving end of this scenario, what would I hope to happen?"

Here is a list of some of my guiding principles that I live by to give you an example of what is important to me, but each of us are free to choose our own. We instinctively know in our hearts what is right and what is wrong for each of us.

My guiding principles:

- To treat others as I wish to be treated
- To be kind and loving to all people.
- To love and serve all the people within my reach, to be a force of love and strength in the world.
- To be honest, trustworthy and faithful in all my relationships.
- To smile and be cheerful.
- To value my body and treat it with the care it deserves.
- To be forgiving. It is not my job to judge others as I have not lived their lives and I don't know how they feel.
- To be grateful for all that I have and all that I am.
- To be polite and well mannered, and to teach my children the same.
- To use good clean language.
- To be easy to talk to and be a good listener
- To be open to being a friend to anyone that needs.
- To take responsibility for the well-being of others within my reach.
- To treat all people as equals.
- To feed myself and others only healthful foods.
- To put myself in the shoes of another to try to understand their point of view or understand why they behave the way they do.

This list can go on and on and we can add to it as we learn and grow into kinder and better people but start to decide today what kind of human being you want to be. In order to be happy and successful in life we first need to know who we want to be and where we are going.

List your top ten guiding principles.

1-
2-
3-
4-
5-
6-
7-
8-
9-
10-

Even when we have our guiding principles in place, we may still make mistakes as none of us are perfect, but we can do our best to remedy our behaviour by apologising and admitting we are wrong or admitting we have behaved in an unacceptable manner. We cannot change the past but we can change ourselves and commit to being better in the future.

When we behave badly or in an unacceptable way, our bodies will tell us immediately. That wave of regret and self-loathing can enter into our bodies and give us that sick feeling, and we literally feel heavier and weighed down with guilt and regret.

Our bodies also immediately tell us when we do something that we know is good. For example, if we see someone struggling with something, let's say there's an elderly lady whose shopping bag has burst open in the street and all her groceries are scattered all around her. If we run to the rescue and help her to gather them up, get a replacement bag for her and make sure she has everything she needs, not only will she feel good that there are good people in the world, but we feel amazing for lifting someone up and being a good human being. We will literally feel on a high, feel lighter and feel totally elated and most likely walk away with a bounce in our step and a great big smile on our face. It's one of the greatest feelings in the world!

So, it's actually up to us how we choose to live our lives by setting our guiding principles firmly in place to lead us to a happier life and a happier heart!

Who Do I Want to Become?

Unless we understand who we are as human beings, how we want life to feel, and what we want to give to others in our lives, we may never discover why we are here or what our true purpose is. We all have a reason for being and we are all part of the universe's plan, but first of all, it's our job to work out who we truly are for ourselves. We have to use our hearts as a guide to uncover our true reason for being and follow our own bliss. Every step forward we take through following our hearts will eventually lead us to our life's greater purpose.

I was very fortunate when I was little because I knew from the age of about three that I wanted to be a hairstylist. I was determined that that was what I would do. I loved doing everyone's hair and making them feel better.

I vividly remember putting curlers in my Auntie Claire's hair and being so small that the only way to reach her was by standing on the back of her chair while she was sitting on it. I don't know which of us loved it more. I can only imagine how 'unique' her hair looked when I was finished.

My mum used to tell stories of me getting my hands on a pair of scissors and trimming all the dolls' hair. My sisters must have been so upset with all the weird and wonderful hairstyles their poor dolls got, but I can't remember them ever complaining.

"It will grow back!" I used to tell my mum. How could she lose her temper with me when I was living my little existence so passionately?

Apart from briefly wanting to be a ballet dancer, I never changed my mind about what I wanted to do. I left school at 16 and went on to college for two years to study hair and beauty. I sailed through the two years and loved every minute. I had gone to see the careers councillor at school previously because I wanted to stay on at school. I felt I wasn't quite ready to leave my friends behind or ready to grow up (I still felt like a little girl and leaving school was a scary thought) but I was advised to leave as I was so determined and fixated on becoming a hairstylist. He said that I would be wasting a year if I stayed at school especially because I was so passionate and sure of what I would do with my life. Even in hindsight, I believe he made the right call.

Even though I was really shy, at aged 14, I went to every single hair salon in my town, there were about six of them at the time, to ask if I could work for them for free on a Saturday sweeping the floor, cleaning and making coffee. I was so nervous about asking but I had to follow my heart. When we want something enough, we breakthrough our fears and barriers that block us because our passion fuels our energy and enthusiasm.

I was turned down by every single one of them but I couldn't understand why. Why would anyone turn away someone that was willing to work for free? I desperately wanted to be a part of that world but I had to trust that it wasn't meant to be at the time. I had to wait until I could leave school and start college. In the meantime, I had to make do with sitting my younger sister in the bath, cutting her hair freestyle, poor girl, but I was determined that one day each of the salons would regret their decision. Rejection didn't put me off, it made me even more determined to succeed.

I got a job offer straight out of college and within six months, at 18 years old, I was made a manager of a salon. I transformed the salon from a small low earning business to being a super busy and popular salon.

It was a great success. I was a great success. And I went from earning £55-a-week wage (well it was a long time ago) to earning around three times that much by the time my commission was added.

All I did was do my job and love every minute of it. I believed then, as I still believe now, that when we do what we love, it's not work. It's spending our days doing what we love and getting paid for it.

I've never been interested in how much money I earn but more interested in how much I love what I do. I believe that whatever we do with love, will be rewarded back to us at the right time. I believe success is living a life that we love, doing what we love, regardless of how much money we earn or how the world labels us and our achievements, as long as it is in alignment with our guiding principles.

At 21, I started my own business/ hairdressing salon with my friend which was so much fun. We had all the freedom we wanted and got to spend every day laughing and joking while doing what we loved most. We stayed late most evenings but not because we were workaholics but because we would continue to laugh and have fun, having races on our fancy hairdressing chairs.

Being a grown-up wasn't so scary after all. Living a happy life has nothing to do with how old we are, whether we are in our teens, twenties, fifties or seventies; it's actually *how* we decide to live that determines the quality of our lives.

At 21, I was still shy within my personal life but when I was working, I came alive. Walking into my salon was like stepping out onto a stage and I loved every minute.

After eight years of having the salon, I stopped loving it and decided to make some changes. My health became a problem as I developed chronic asthma so changes needed to be made. I sold up and began another journey. This time I had to work on my health and on myself. Because of a near-death experience, I now realised how precious life was and knew that I had to change my life and my health.

There are times in life that things just have to change, we need to move on and grow. We can decide to accept life's challenges and struggle on or we can change ourselves and the direction that we are going in, and move forward on a new path. Our dreams change and evolve as we do, so it's up to us whether to accept an unhappy life or go chasing after our new dreams and make new life plans. The point is that we can choose.

I had loved hairdressing, and making others feel better, not only through making them look better but by having wonderful conversations and creating deep and meaningful relationships with my clients. It was hard to leave but I knew it was time to move on.

To understand what we want, we first need to know how we want to *feel* about ourselves and our lives. I knew that I wanted to be healthy, to no longer struggle to breathe and to live every day with love. Health and love for life were, and still are, one of my main priorities and they are what drive me.

Let's say for example that our goal in life is to become rich so we can have all the material things we want in life.

How do we expect to feel as a result of being rich? We have to ask ourselves *why* we want to be rich. Do we think it will make us happy? If so, why?

- Is it to feel important?
- To feel respected?
- To be seen as being 'as good as', or better than, others?
- To be able to feed your family?
- Is it to be able to change the world somehow?
- To make a difference in the lives of others?
- Is it because you want to do whatever you please with your life?

Understanding why we want what we want can help us to move in the direction we want to go.

What is it that you want to achieve in your life, why and how do you want to feel about yourself and your achievements?

Why do you think firemen want to be firemen? Doctors want to be doctors? Ministers want to be ministers? Movie stars want to be movie stars?

Each of them had a feeling attached to why they do what they do.

Do you think firemen became firemen because they like the uniform or because they want to play a heroic role in life? Would they put their lives in danger because of the pension plan that is provided or because they want to save lives? Did they choose their profession to look cool or to be respected by society?

We are all unique and so no two people will have the same reasons for choosing what we choose to be in life. Our motives will differ greatly, but before we decide who we want to be, we need to know why.

Once we know *why* we want something and our desire is compelling, we fix determination and passion in our hearts and minds which will fuel us to keep moving forward and never give up when things get tough.

Let's say that a wannabe fireman doesn't get into the Fire Service due to health issues, does that mean his life purpose and dream is shattered? Absolutely not! When we know *how* we want to *feel* and *why*, we can find other ways to fulfil our life's purpose.

In fact, when life doesn't go to plan, I believe that it is God giving us a nudge to help us to change direction. When something is not meant to be then the universe will tell us. We only have to trust that even when we have given something or someone our all, and it still doesn't work out, then that is what is meant to be.

It will all work out for the best in the end.

Looking back, I wanted to be a hairdresser because lifting others was in my heart and soul. It was a way for me to express my creativity, as well as help others to look good and feel good. When I saw the look on my clients' faces after I had made them look good, I felt overjoyed that I had the capacity to improve someone's life in some way. When we look better, we feel better. Fact. Have you ever bounced out of a salon feeling like the bee's knees? Well, as a hairstylist, I felt like I was making a difference and playing my part. Very rarely did anyone feel worse after spending some time with me and that was the *feeling* that I loved. I wanted to help others feel happy and good about themselves.

I outgrew hairdressing but my reason for my present work is the same. To help others to feel good about themselves mind, body and soul. That is what makes me happy and brings me joy. I love nothing more than seeing other people smile, especially if I have played a part in it.

Asking ourselves good questions means that we will find good answers which will help to steer us towards a full and happy life. We have to be honest and open with ourselves in order to know what we truly want. There are no right or wrong answers but it's important that we ask the right questions.

Who Do I Want to Become?

1. If I could choose to have one super power in this world, what would it be, and how would I use my power to improve the world?

a. My super power would be…

b. I would use my power to…

2. How do I want other people to feel when they are around me? List below with a reason why you want others to feel this way (use the table as a guide and add your own personal idea)

Safe	Equal to me	Like they matter
Loved	Significant	Relaxed
Cared for	Joyful	Understood
Happy	At peace	Valued
Lifted	Special	Heard/Listened to

a.

b.

c.

d.

e.

f.

g.

h.

i.

j.

3. What impression do I want to leave someone after they have met me for the first time? What would I hope they would say about me when I am gone? List below using the table as a guide:

Kind	Passionate	Sincere
Sweet	Honest	Warm
Thoughtful	Clever	Wise
Cheerful	Intelligent	Funny
Happy	Interesting	Hilarious
Chatty	Open minded	Playful
Easy going	Outgoing	Hard working
Enthusiastic	Easy to talk to	Courageous

a.   b.

c.   d.

e.   f.

g.   h.

i.   j.

4. Using the same list above as a guide, write a list of qualities that you would like to see in other people in your life?

a.   b.

c.   d.

e.   f.

g.   h.

i.   j.

5. The big question is: "Am I the person that I want to be?" Explain why this is.

Being Myself

Human beings are born into this world as pure and perfect beings and we are all equal, no matter what kind of family we are born into. Whether we are born into royalty or into poverty, we were all pure and perfect. Some of us lead privileged lives and want for nothing, and some live lives surrounded by great adversity and struggle, but again we are all equal in value.

What we are, or have, on the surface and what we are surrounded by is no indication of the kind of people we are. What makes an incredible human being and makes them valuable is what is in a person's heart and soul, how they love, and how they treat others.

We can sometimes get lost in the big wide world out there and therefore follow what others are doing because it's the '*in*' thing to do, but more often than not, we are being led in a different direction from where we need to be, in essence, away from who we really are. So, before we go any further it's important that we stop, reset our compass and actually work out where we are headed.

Once we know who we are, and what kind of person we want to be, we then have to make sure that we stay on track so we don't get lost or lose ourselves on the path. People and things cannot change who we are or lead us astray, it's all down to us and the choices that we make. When we live our lives by our guiding principles and make the right choices for us personally, then we are always on the right path.

Whenever we come to a fork in the road in all aspects of life and wonder which road to take, we have to ask ourselves: "Which one is going to lead me to being my best self and which one will lead me away from being the best version of me?"

We also have to ask ourselves 'Why?' when we are making certain choices.

- Why would this be a good choice to make?
- Is it because I think I ought to, to perhaps be liked by others and to fit in, or is it because that is what is best for me?
- Will it take me to where I want to be, or lead me away from it?
- Is this truly what I want?
- When I look back at my life when I am old will I be glad that I took this path or will I regret it?
- Am I choosing this for the right reasons that will take me where I need to go, or am I doing it to please others?

This covers all areas in life. In our relationship choices, in our food and health choices, in our character-building choices, in our career choices etc. When we know exactly the kind of person we want to be and know our own strength and power, we will make the right choices that can take us there.

Let me tell you about a story I heard a few years ago concerning some students studying in Japan.

Many years ago, there was a young man named John and he and his two friends, had each applied to get into a prestigious business school in Japan. They knew exactly what they wanted to do and were determined to be a great success and this was the school that would get them there. When they were accepted, they were overjoyed as all their hard work was finally paying off. This was an opportunity of a lifetime.

In the first few weeks of school, all the students from all over the world were just getting to know each other and these three boys were invited to a rooftop party one evening. They were keen to meet up with some of the other students on a personal level and make some new friends so they happily went along. It started off a lovely evening as they were mingling with all these new people but as the evening went on, the three friends started noticing that drugs were being passed around and started to feel uneasy. John didn't feel right and decided to leave the party and call it a night. He just knew it wasn't his scene so he made the decision to leave but before doing so he turned to his two friends and encouraged them to leave with him. One of them had the compelling argument that as long as *he* didn't take them, he would be okay, but John convinced his other friend to leave with him.

As they were exiting the building, the police ran past them and raided the building and everyone at the party was detained. Some of the students were arrested and the others were sent back to their own countries in disgrace by the school, John's friend included. His whole future was changed because he chose not to walk away when he had the chance. He may not have been taking the drugs but because he chose to accept the environment he was in, and the people he was associated with, he missed out on an incredible opportunity for a better future.

John and his other friend completed their studies and consequently went on to have affluent careers and achieve all their personal goals. Their lives went according to plan because they made the right choice.

When we know who we want to be, we have to listen to our inner selves, our gut feelings and stand strong. When we live in accordance with our guiding principles, we will be able to guide ourselves through life instead of being led by what everyone else is doing. We may have to stand alone, walk away and be judged for it but what is important is that we make our choices and take responsibility for our own lives. When things don't work out, we cannot blame others because *we* made the choices whether they were good or bad. Nobody can make us do anything! We choose our own destiny!

Later on in the book, we will work on painting a picture of your future self, to have a vision of the person you want to be many years from now but in the meantime think about the people that have influenced you in your life so far.

We are all influenced by the people around us, just as we influence them, so it's important that we decide whether to be a good influence or a bad one. This book is to open your awareness of the power that you have over your own life and to help you to realise your worth as a human being, but it is also to realise our own moral obligation to lift others up as we grow.

Instead of running ahead in life striving to win, we have to move forward leading, supporting and encouraging those that are within our reach to be better and happier as we journey through life together, no matter how old we are.

All of us want to live in a happier world and want to play our part so we can choose whether to be leaders in life and make a difference, or just to be followers.

Which role do you choose?

1. Who was, or possibly still is, the biggest influence for good in your life when you were younger and how did they treat you?

For example. Apart from my parents, I had my Auntie Claire who I loved so much. She was a family friend but she was like a grandmother to me.

2. How did you/do you feel about him/her and what makes you feel that way about them?

Example. Auntie Claire meant the world to me and I wanted to be with her all the time. I felt loved and special in her presence. I felt like she could see my soul. She was so kind and lovingly taught me about good manners, how to be a good person and how to treat others.

3. How do you want to show up in the lives of others? (What kind of influence do you want to be?)

Example: I want to be a good person and a friend to anyone that needs me. To be a force of love in the lives of others for them to feel that they are valued and never alone. To be a light, and to pass on that light to everyone I meet, so they will never feel alone in the dark.

Love Lesson #2
My Self-Worth

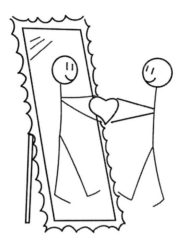

"We are each stars in the universe and we all shine in our own way."

One of the main reasons for writing this book was to help young people to realise their self-worth and to help them to love themselves and their lives more.

I believe that the majority of our problems stem from the fact that we are not loving ourselves or valuing ourselves enough.

I'm not talking about looking in the mirror and thinking 'WOW what a hottie!' or chanting 'I love you, I love you, I love you!', I'm talking about truly learning to love and appreciate ourselves deep within our souls for who we are. To know and understand that we are one with the universe and that we each have a reason for being here.

We can look in the mirror and repeatedly tell ourselves that we are loveable and beautiful beings, but unless we truly feel it, we are wasting our breath.

I'll never forget the story that my mum told me when she was a young girl and nearly drowned.

Even though she could not swim very well, she loved the beach and one day while she was playing in the shallow water, she saw someone further out waving and screaming for help. Because of her selfless nature and love for others, she ran in to save this poor girl without even thinking of herself and her own inability to swim. Only when she got further out, and out of her depth, did she realise that she was in terrible danger. She was helpless and she could do nothing, not just to save the drowning girl, but also to save herself. Thankfully a man had witnessed my mum's heroic act (well attempt at it) and managed to jump in to save them both.

When my mum recalled the story, she said, "It never even crossed my mind that I couldn't swim, I just had to do something. I had to jump in to save her... and I almost died!"

I believe that this is a good analogy for life and for love. We often jump into relationships even when we don't know what we are doing.

Before we jump into the sea, whether to swim or to save a life, we first need to learn how to swim ourselves. We may have seen others do it or we may have a minimum level of understanding, but until we actually do the work and learn the skill with our very own bodies, no amount of knowledge, without putting it into actual practice, can keep us or others safe.

Well, the same goes for life. Before we jump into the sea of life and relationships, we need to know we have sufficient knowledge and love for ourselves. If we jump into life thinking that we can save others by loving them, or vice versa, we too could be in danger of losing a part of ourselves. Without self-love and worth we may compromise our health, our well-being, our existing relationships and our life's purpose.

Self-love is the key to all the wonderful treasures of life and we all have access to it, but first, we need to plant the seeds, water them often and spend time throughout our lives continually nurturing those seeds of love to allow them to grow.

If we want to be a source of love in the lives of others, we must have a natural reservoir of love already within us. After all, we cannot share with others what we do not have ourselves.

- If we loved ourselves and truly valued the gift of our healthy bodies, would we fuel them with things that we know are harmful to our well-being?
- If we truly loved ourselves, would we say unkind things about ourselves such as "I'm ugly, I'm fat, or I'm not good enough or smart enough"?
- If we truly valued our lives would we waste time and energy living unhappy lives trying to fit in with the world's and others' ideas of what happiness looks like?
- If we valued our time upon the earth would we waste time comparing ourselves to others instead of embracing our inner selves and making the most of every day by living life with joy and purpose?
- If we valued our gifts and talents would we waste them by doing nothing to develop and nurture them to use them to improve not only our own lives, but also the lives of others?

Unfortunately, there seems to be much sadness and depression in society today, and the more I speak to people, the more I realise that most people are struggling which breaks my heart. They are living day by day, enduring life, but not living with joy.

It upsets me because I can see an emptiness in people that desperately needs to be filled. They are starving for love and connection not only with others, but with themselves and are in need of answers to why they are here. I know this because I was one of those people and I know what it feels like. Now I do all that I can to ease the suffering in others and help them, just as I helped myself.

In the world today, if we are not consciously aware of it, we can easily get sucked into a superficial digital and material world that is foreign to our basic instincts as human beings and we can be left feeling lost, inadequate, not good enough, not worthy enough, not rich enough, not smart enough or not attractive enough.

We suffer from depression and anxiety because in this world of technology we have lost touch with who we are as individuals, why we are here, and what our purpose is as human beings. We no longer connect with others through real conversation and face-to-face interaction.

I can see this world and the people within it becoming lost in the fog of confusion and I have made it my mission to help them. Without the awareness of self, they can get lost between living a life they think they *should* live and a life that they intuitively desire to live as a human being.

My mission is to help them to have clarity of heart and mind, and to know why they are here. To understand what is truly important in life and for them to feel whole within themselves.

When we open ourselves up to an awareness to who we really are on a deeper level and what our purpose is, we can find the true treasures of life.

We can be and do whatever we decide in life but we first have to love ourselves enough to start. God created us all the way he did for a reason, and we are all unique and individual. When we give up comparing ourselves with others, we are free to be our true and imperfect selves. Once we understand that, we can begin to love the best version of who we are already and not who we think we ought to be.

When we look at ourselves in the mirror, we often look for all the imperfections. We focus on the flaws and begin to compare ourselves to others instead of focusing on what truly matters. None of us are perfect externally or internally and we never will be, so the first thing we need to do is let go of perfection. People's ideas of beauty are so vast that we could never be beautiful in everyone's eyes. NEVER! So, the sooner we let go of the myth of perfection in every area of our lives, the sooner we can start living a fulfilling and happy life.

We all have a picture in our own minds of what a perfect human looks like and if we don't look like that picture, we begin to feel bad about ourselves. Yes, some may have perfectly defined features according to our own perceptions but true beauty is found in a smile and in an openly loving heart. If we judge others by what they look like, then it is only natural to think that others will judge us in the same way. So, we have to ask ourselves:

"If I determine the value of a person by the way they look, what does that say about me? And if I don't, why would others judge me for the way I look?"

The truth is, and what we all instinctively know is, that the outside has nothing to do with who we are and what we are worth. The old adage "Don't judge a book by its cover" means we have to delve into the pages of the book before we decide whether we like it or not, or if it is of any value to us. Well, the same goes when we look at the outer shell of a person. Our bodies that are made of flesh and bone are just vessels in which to house our true treasure and worth, our souls, but we also have to take care of our bodies in the best possible way that we can. After all, we cannot live life without them.

If we judge ourselves by the way we look, we therefore assume that others value us in the same way.

Unfortunately, some people in this world are losing sight of what really matters, and will judge us for the way we look but that only tells us about who they are and the work that they need to do on themselves. It says nothing about us.

If *we* are *being* that person that is judging others, we need to look deep within ourselves and decide if that is the kind of person we want to be. We are not perfect and we all make mistakes but we can always change our ways and change our thinking to become the people we want to be. We *build* character, it is not all in our DNA.

The only thing that truly matters in life is love. Love for humanity, love for our fellow beings that we are walking through life with and love for our very reason for being. We have each been given the gift of love in our hearts and we can either embrace it in all its splendour and use it to create a masterpiece of our lives, or we can lock it away, not put any value on who we really are and make do with whatever comes our way. But when we truly love ourselves and the gift we have been given of life, we will see our lives and see ourselves as vessels of love and do what we can to make a difference to the world. Our true value is in how we treat ourselves and others, and life will reward us with a peaceful heart and the true treasures of life.

I share my knowledge and understanding because I have been there. Been in that place in my mind where I was never enough. I wish that I could have had this knowledge when I was young, to have books like this to guide me through life, to understanding who I was then, which is why I have created this book as a guide for others.

My Appearance

Unfortunately, I spent most of my life thinking I was ugly for many reasons.

Firstly, because I sucked my thumb until I was 15 and every time my mum looked at me, she commented on how ugly I looked with my thumb in my mouth. She obviously didn't say it to hurt me; she most likely thought that it would make me stop, but it in fact made me more insecure which in turn made me turn to the comfort of thumb sucking.

Secondly, I didn't eat properly until the age of seven. Mealtimes were a nightmare for both my mum and me because she desperately wanted me to eat as I was so thin. She used to say, "You are too skinny, if only you would eat more, then you would be beautiful like your sisters." Again, she never meant to hurt me but I took all the criticism to heart and believed that I was not good enough or as good as my sisters.(Consequently, both my sisters became overweight as they were praised for their eating habits).

Thirdly, every time my mum looked in a mirror or saw a photo of herself, she used to comment on how ugly she was, yet everyone commented on how I was the double of my mum. This just confirmed the vision I had of myself. I used to look at my mum and think she was ugly too because I had heard it so many times and I found myself falling into the same habit of telling myself how ugly I was.

As a little girl, I thought being beautiful was important. I believed that life would be better and that being beautiful would make me happy. After all, that's what all the fairy tales and films implied. I dreamt of one day being like Cinderella instead of one of the ugly sisters and a handsome prince would find me.

I eventually found my prince charming but I still felt like the same worthless

Cinderella deep within myself. I thought that being loved by someone else would fill the emptiness inside me but the only person that could do that was me.

Each of us are responsible for our own inner happiness and no one can make us happy, or unhappy for that matter. We choose how we feel. We can choose happiness or misery. We can choose to see the good in ourselves and in others, or choose to see all the bad. There is good and bad in all of us but when we are kind and loving towards ourselves and others, and choose to focus on nourishing the good within us, then we can continue to grow and become better every day.

I used to believe that someone else would make me happy even though I was unhappy with myself, but that is like someone else eating healthily for us and hoping to be nourished by it. We have to feed our own bodies healthful foods to be nourished and we also need to feed our minds and hearts the right fuel to nourish our souls.

I had this need to feel loved as a sign of my self-worth but I was looking in the wrong places. If I had openly spoken about my lack of self-love then, I'm sure someone would have told me otherwise but I thought it was normal. Lots of my friends were the same. Insecure and feeling like they weren't good enough, pretty enough or clever enough.

I had a fixation in my mind that I was not enough and I had no idea how to change that. It took me many years and a lot of soul searching before I felt truly loved.

I had two wonderful children and felt so loved by them but I couldn't shake off that feeling of self-doubt and lack of love for myself.

Looking back at my youth now, I realise that I became a hairstylist as a way to make others feel beautiful and good about themselves. We naturally create what we need to feel within ourselves. For example, if we want to feel loved we give others all the love that we want to receive. If we want to feel safe, we create a safe environment. If we want to feel beautiful, we help others to feel beautiful and so on. I believe that because I knew how it felt to feel bad about myself, I did all I could to prevent it from happening to others. It makes perfect sense. I became a hairstylist to lift others up and to make them feel good.

Because I valued myself for the way I looked it meant I had no self-worth. When I changed my perspective, my point of view, I could see myself from the inside out and only then did I realise where self-worth and self-love really reside. Within my heart and soul.

If we don't love ourselves enough when others tell us we are not good enough, attractive enough or clever enough (as they do), we may actually believe them. By changing our perspective from looking at ourselves from the outside, to looking at ourselves from the inside, we are able to see and feel the true value of who we are. I know this is nothing new and nothing we didn't know already but do we actually put it into practice? Beauty really comes from within and shines out on our faces, it doesn't come from perfectly toned bodies and a flawless face.

Think about someone elderly that you love. Someone that has lived out their lives and it shows on their face. A grandparent or old relative perhaps. Do you see them as unattractive, wrinkly and ugly or do you see the beauty in their eyes and smile? Do you love their soft skin, warm embrace and feel so much love in their company? It's absolutely who we are on the inside that counts and no matter what we look like we have to love every single part of us.

Due to never feeling good enough when I was young, I never felt whole and therefore spent my life looking for others to make me complete. We hear all these beautiful sayings such as :

"He completes me."
"She is my better half."
"She is my life."
"Together we are one."
"I can't live without him."

As romantic as these may sound, they all imply that without someone to love us, we are not whole. That we are incomplete. 'THAT IS NOT THE CASE!!!'

We are all complete and whole within ourselves and we don't *need someone else* to fill the empty space in our hearts, *we* need to.

Once we do so, we are then ready to find another person to take this journey through life with us. To go through life together growing, learning and sharing our time and love. If we go into relationships with an idea that they will make us whole, how will we feel when we are apart? Broken and empty again? Worthless and incomplete?

We have to take responsibility for becoming whole within ourselves before we can give ourselves to another. It is not fair to expect another person to fill an emptiness within us or for us to feel we have to do the same. True love is two whole and complete beings that have openly chosen each other as a life partner. Love is not finding someone to love us, take care of us and make us happy. That is our job and our own responsibility.

One of the biggest lessons I have learned in life is that other people cannot make us happy, and we cannot make others happy either. We are each responsible for our own happiness.

Being with them can make us feel happy and loving them can make us feel happy but they themselves are not in charge of our happiness. We are!

So how do we learn to love and value ourselves?

1. To be our own best friend.
2. To know that the only person that we 'need' to be loved by, is ourselves.
3. To realise that the secret to living is giving.
4. To care less of what other people think of us.
5. To work on growing our gifts and talents, and sharing them.
6. To believe that we can make a difference in the world, one person at a time.
7. To feed our minds, bodies and souls only things that will nourish them.
8. To do things that make ourselves feel useful and of value to others.
9. To see ourselves through the eyes of those that love us unconditionally.
10. To step forward out of our comfort zones and into our light.

To be our own best friend.
The majority of us are too hard on ourselves and we are our own worst critic. We catch ourselves saying things like I look ugly in this or I'm so fat or my clothes don't look good on me' etc. but would you ever say that to your best friend? If you did, you wouldn't stay best friends for long I'm sure. So, start to talk kindly to yourself and ask yourself what you would say about yourself if you were your own best

friend.

Would you accept it if someone else spoke to you the way you speak to yourself saying things like "You are useless. You don't deserve that. You look awful"? I doubt you would accept such criticism without feeling bitter or upset, yet you allow yourself to say such things. From today on make a conscious effort to only use kind and loving words when talking to yourself, and about yourself. I'm not saying that we have to look at ourselves and chant: "You are perfect. You are gorgeous. You are spectacular. You are better than others." I mean be kind and thoughtful in your words and thoughts towards yourself and imagine that you are talking openly and honestly with your best friend. For example, "My skin isn't as good as it could be so it would be good to drink more water and cut out the fast foods" or "I may not have the body I want but I know it is my responsibility so I will start taking better care of myself" or "I know I can do better so I'll put more effort into it."

The negative words will still pop into mind and out of your mouth from time to time but apologise to yourself and say something nice in its place. You deserve to be treated with love and kindness, especially by you.

It may be an idea to write down every time you hear yourself say something unkind to give you an idea of how often you do it. Being consciously aware of your behaviour and your negative self-talk will help you to make the changes necessary to start to be your very own best friend.

To know that the only person that we need to be loved by, is ourselves.

The one person that will be by your side and be with you every single day of your life is the person that you see every time you look in the mirror. They say life is short but imagine spending a whole lifetime with someone you don't even love. So, the sooner you learn to love and accept yourself, the better and happier you will be. We want others to love us and accept us for who we really are, so we have to do the same.

If you don't like who you are as a person, then do something about it and be the person you wish to be around.

If you are being your true and authentic self you can only like yourself. It's only when we start going against what our guiding principles are that we are led away from the kind of person that we want to be. Does that make sense? Let me explain. I believe that if we don't love ourselves, it is because we are not living in alignment with who we really are, or in other words, we are not being ourselves. We often put on a face or an act in order to fit in and be liked by others but wouldn't it make more sense to just be ourselves and like ourselves? We will always come across people that will never 'get us' or see things from our point of view but being liked by others isn't the problem, is it?

It's actually loving and accepting ourselves, the real us, that makes us happy. For example, if we don't like a person, it's usually because we don't like a personality trait that they have, or we have decided, without even knowing them, that they are not our 'cup of tea'. True? Perhaps they are loud and full of life but we find them annoying, or alternatively too quiet and boring for our liking. But if we are not being the kind of person that is to *our* liking then we are not being ourselves.

Perhaps we dislike people that are loud and full of life because that is who we are deep down but are too afraid to just be ourselves. Perhaps they annoy us because they are brave enough to be themselves and reminds us that we are not.

So be brave by being yourself, even if you have to stand alone. If those in your circle don't like the real you then so be it. Those that do love you, will love you still, and those that don't, never really did. Trust yourself and live by your own guiding principles that you believe make a good human being. By doing so, the right people will enter your life and your self-love and self-worth will grow.

Listen and follow the true goodness of your heart and it will lead you to that love. Once we learn to love ourselves and value ourselves as human beings, others will naturally follow.

"The secret to living is giving."

The incredible coach Tony Robbins uses this phrase all the time and I agree with him 100%. The secret to living a happy life is not what we can get from life, it's what we can give to life. We feel fulfilled as we serve others and do all we can to lift others up. When we receive a gift or buy ourselves something new, we feel great for a while but when we do things for others and see the joy and happiness on their faces, it brings long-lasting fulfilment and pure joy to our hearts. We all have the ability to be kind and loving, and to share our time and love with others, so let's do it.

When we focus on making others smile, we feel genuine happiness and our self-worth begins to grow. We realise the power that we have in our own hands to make others smile and to make a difference in the world, which in turn makes us smile.

It is the secret to life. Money, people and material things come and go but love and kindness stay with us forever and is the very essence and fuel for a happy life.

All it takes is for us to be aware of everyone that crosses our path and to ask ourselves: "How can I make them smile?"

We don't need lots of time, money or resources to change lives, it just takes love and small acts of kindness.

- A Smile
- A phone call to a relative
- A note
- A compliment
- A kind word
- A text message to reconnect with an old friend
- Visiting an elderly neighbour
- Taking some healthy cookies to a friend in need of cheering up
- Chatting to an elderly person in the supermarket
- Offering to babysit
- Doing jobs around the house without being asked
- Offering to cut someone's grass for them
- Seeking out those in need of a friend

There are endless possibilities of ways we can serve others in our own home, in our neighbourhood and in our community. It doesn't only put smiles on their faces but builds a deep love for others within ourselves and for our lives. Keeping our eyes, ears and hearts open with a willingness to serve brings peace of mind and heart in everyone.

To care less of what other people think of us.

When we know who we are, and love the people we are becoming, then it really doesn't matter what others say or think.

- If they think that we are unkind but we know we are not, so what?
- If they think we are an attention seeker but we know we are not, so what?
- If they think we are lazy but we know that we are not, so what?
- If they say we are selfish but we know that we are not, so what?
- If they call us stupid but we know we are not, so what?

We may act in these ways from time to time but it's not who we are. We may be lazy at times or say stupid things for example but that doesn't make us lazy or stupid.

It is actually not a problem what others say or think about us unless we make it a problem. If we know who we are, know that we are being our best selves and know what is in our hearts then what others say about us is only their *opinion* and not fact.

Others can only offend us if we believe what they are saying is true.

For example, if someone was to call you a blue alien, would you be offended? No, you wouldn't because you know 100% that you are not a blue alien, true? But if someone was to call you nasty or stupid, would you be offended? Most likely, but why? It's because you would believe there is some truth in their words.

You would begin to question yourself and your worth, but if you know who you are and know you are a good and loving person, nothing that anyone else says matters.

For example, I received an email when I was training to become a life coach from a female that I have never met before saying that she thought I shouldn't become a life coach because I was an attention seeker and flirt, and that they are not good qualities to be doing that kind of work. I was so shocked and upset initially and just cried. How could someone say such things that were not true about me? Then I asked myself: "Am I an attention seeker and a flirt? What did I do that was so wrong?"

When I started to unravel the thoughts in my head, I realised that I was asking myself the wrong questions.

I know who I am and what my intentions for life are. I am an openly loving person with everyone and if I can improve someone's life by telling them I care, I will. My heart is pure and all that I do is to spread love and kindness wherever I can. So why am I getting upset about this email… it says nothing about me, but is someone's opinion of me which is so far from the truth.

Because I know myself and love the person I am constantly growing into, I was able to ask different questions such as:

- Does it even matter what people think of me? No.
- Am I being my best self? Yes.
- Do the people I love know who I am? Yes.
- Are the opinions of others going to stop me from living my purpose? No.
- Can I help people to love themselves and their lives more? Yes.
- Will I continue to be openly loving to all? Yes.

Then there is no problem. This lady was judging me without even knowing me and felt the need to tell me how she felt. I sent her loving thoughts and an email saying that I was sorry that she felt that way but if she wanted to meet me for a chat, I would be happy for her to get to know me and realise that I am not who she thinks I am.

I am grateful for that email because I learned something new about myself that day which made it a good day for me. I learned that people won't always understand me or believe in me but I will never stop being me, never stop loving openly and never stop caring for others. It's who I am.

That evening, I told my husband about what had happened and he said, "Never ever change, never stop being you!"

To work on growing our gifts and talents, and sharing them.

In order for us to realise our worth we need to keep growing and keep improving who we are as human beings as well as working on our gifts and talents.

We all have God-given natural gifts and talents and they are usually exactly what we love doing, but without developing and working on them, we are not tapping into our potential.

Some of our gifts are clear and obvious and others take time and years to manifest themselves, but we all have them.

For example, maybe you have an amazing singing voice or alternatively an enormous desire to work at becoming a great singer and performer. Both take work and practise and you can equally succeed with either but the important thing is that we work on what we love doing and not let our talents go to waste. Alternatively, your gift could be more subtle, such as your ability to make people smile, or perhaps children love you and you love them. We have to dedicate time and energy to working on what we love and what makes our hearts shine. We have to develop our passions and seek out opportunities to do what we love.

In the world of technology and media we can often get distracted from our true reason for being, so always make your God-given gifts a priority. Your future self will thank you for it.

When we do things we are good at, it helps to build our self-worth and we realise that we have a lot to offer the world. We each have so much to give, in so many different ways but we have to listen to our hearts, believe in ourselves and do what we love.

If we do what we love we never have to work a day in our lives. Every day of the week can be a Funday!

To believe that we can make a difference in the world, one person at a time.

It doesn't matter who we are or what our gifts and talents are, we all have the ability to make a difference.

All of us can change lives in some way, even just by being a friend. By showing up in life with an open heart and open arms to allow new people in. We need to open our eyes to the needs of the people that are around us and take responsibility for others that are on this same journey through life.

The real treasures in life are love, kindness and connection, and we can only be measured by how much we are willing to share these treasures. Everything else is extra. We have nothing if we have perfect bodies and flawless complexions if we don't possess love and kindness. It means nothing to have a wardrobe full of beautiful clothes, a cool car and live in a fabulous house if we don't possess love, kindness and connection.

So, no matter who we are, what we look like, how many qualifications we have, how old we are or what our gifts are, the one thing that we possess that is of any true value is our love for others.

When we know and believe that we can make a difference in the lives of others, we will realise that we have so much to give. The world needs kinder and more loving people to be examples of love so it is our duty and moral obligation to be those people and to spread light in the world. There is a lot of darkness in the world but the more we shine, the brighter this world will be. When we brighten lives, we will understand our worth.

To feed our minds, bodies and souls only things that will nourish them.

How we treat our bodies, minds and souls is an indication of how much worth we put on ourselves.

If we treat the gift of our bodies as if they are no value, then they will be of no value to us. Imagine you got a gorgeous new puppy and you were fully responsible for taking care of it. To ensure his well-being, you need to take him out for long walks to get his exercise three times a day, make sure he is fed the right foods in the right proportions to nourish him, and provide him with sufficient water. If you don't take care of him, there is nobody else to do it for you, so what do you do? Do you do what needs to be done to ensure his well-being or do you ignore your duties and just feed him junk foods, sugary drinks, don't take him out for walks and neglect him? How do you think the puppy would feel physically and how much love would he feel for you?

Now think of your own health and well-being. You know what you need to do to make the best of yourself and your health and well-being but are you taking responsibility for yourself by providing your body with sufficient healthy foods, water, exercise and self-care? If not why not? Do you value the life of a puppy above that of your own life? Just as a puppy won't thank you for feeling rotten, neither will you thank yourself for allowing yourself to be treated badly by being neglected. It makes sense, doesn't it? How can you feel of worth and like who you are when you are neglecting your own sense of well-being?

The same goes for our minds and our souls which we will go into later in the book but when we feed ourselves the right fuel, we function better and feel better about who we are. We feel good that we are taking responsibility for our lives and health which in turn builds our self-worth.

To do things that make ourselves feel useful and of value to others.

When speaking to my children about this subject my son said that when he does certain jobs around the house it builds his self-worth. He said that when he cuts the grass for example, he feels like he is being useful and therefore feels a valuable asset to our family. He feels good about himself knowing that he has done a good job and that he is recognised for doing so.

If we spend our lives only thinking of ourselves, only doing things to better our lives and only doing things that we want to do, we can lose our sense of worth. I have always pushed my children to do chores around the house; in fact, I insist it is part of their lives because I know that by doing chores, they are building self-competence as well as self-confidence. To have that feeling of accomplishment at completing a job and feeling pleased with themselves. My daughter loves cooking and gets so excited about serving her delicious creations. She is an amazing cook and creates new and exciting dishes without following recipes (she gets that from me). In fact, she often talks about wanting to be a chef when she grows up because she loves the feeling of making others feel good when eating her delicious foods.

Doing things that make us feel of use to others lifts us up and allows us to feel significant and of worth. Feeling significant in our lives is one of our basic needs as a human being.

Some feel significant by acting or dressing a certain way that catches the eyes of others, some strive to be the best at something to feel significant, some even use their depression as a way to feel significant (although in a negative way) but the best way to feel of worth *and* significant is through our good works and kind deeds.

To see ourselves through the eyes of those that love us unconditionally.

Who truly loves us no matter how we look, how we behave or what we do in our lives?

As a mother, I know that no matter what my kids say or do, I love them with all my heart and soul, and I will always love them. Sometimes they drive me crazy but they are my world. Just as most children are in their parents' eyes. When I was a child myself, I often felt unloved. I did not understand the concept of unconditional love, to love someone regardless of their behaviour or their actions. I felt unloved because I didn't feel I was enough. Good enough, pretty enough or clever enough. I had told my immature mind that my sisters were wonderful but I wasn't because I always got into trouble with my parents and they didn't. I thought my parents didn't love me because they were continually telling me off for some reason or another. I had managed to convince myself that if they loved me, they wouldn't be telling me off which is such nonsense. I carried this lack of love throughout my childhood and even into adulthood which ate away at my self-worth.

We all have times of conflict and disagreement within our families because we are all individuals and we all have our own ideas and opinions in life, but that does not mean that we are not loved. Not even for a second. We may have different ideas of what love looks, sounds and feels like but love is love. Once we define what love is for ourselves, we will know what love means to us and will treat others the way we want to be treated, and love others as we want to be loved.

If I was to describe who I am in one word, my word would be LOVE.

My life revolves around loving others and this is why I do what I do. I genuinely care about others and their well-being. It's just who I am and I am the right person to do this job.

Someone once told me that they did not know that someone like me even existed in the world. I took it as a compliment but they could have meant it in a different way, LOL, they could have meant that they hadn't realised that someone as naive as me existed, but I decided to accept it as a compliment. I am who I am, take me or leave me; love me or hate me, either way I will continue to love you. I didn't feel loved as a child because my idea of love was so different. What does love mean to you?

This is my definition of love:

"When we love another human being, it is an emotion that we feel in the depths of our soul, a feeling that we want the very best for that person. That their well-being is important to us, that they are happy and feel at peace, that they feel valued, know that they are not alone and that we are there for them. We have a desire to do all that we can to make their lives better and happier regardless of how they feel about us or what we get back in return."

This is how I feel about love. This is how I feel about my children, my husband, my family and friends, and about every single person that is within my reach.

Yes, I know I am weird but I also love myself and I am happy with my weirdness. I am me, and that makes me happy because I am being my true self.

My point is that for me, a part of loving someone means taking responsibility for their well-being, not giving them what they want to make them happy when we know it is not the best thing for them. Let me give you an example.

When I was growing up my mum used to make me do housework and at times (I am ashamed to say), I hated her for it. I thought she was cruel and unkind because my friends didn't have to do what I had to. They were out playing while I was cleaning or ironing. I felt as though my mum didn't love me as much as my friends' mums loved them ('Cinderella syndrome' LOL... I was a princess at heart).

Only as I grew up did I realise *why* my mum made me do so much. I grew up unafraid of hard work and developed a good work ethic. I didn't get what I wanted then but I learned that with hard work and determination I could have whatever I wanted in life.

The reality is that life doesn't give us what we want, we have to work for it.

And when we work for it and get it, it brings us a great sense of achievement.

My mum had always loved me but instead of running around tending to all my wants and needs, she taught me about life and how to survive. So, when we don't get what we want in life and our parents stop us from doing something or having something, we have to ask ourselves whether it is for our own good. We may not understand their reasoning and we don't have to, but we do have to trust them. Obviously, there will be exceptions to this way of thinking but when we know we are loved and are treated well, we have to trust that it is for the best. None of us are perfect and as parents, we may make mistakes, but we have to do what we believe to be the best thing for our children.

When we see ourselves through the eyes and hearts of those that love us, whether our parents, grandparents or other family members, we will know that we are loved and that they can see us for the true worth that we are, which in turn helps us to understand our value in their lives.

To step forward out of our comfort zones and into our light.

Taking the journey from childhood to adulthood is no easy feat with all the physical and emotional growth that is going on, but one thing to always remember is that *we* have the power to create the lives that we desire. Our happiness levels are not limited by our circumstances, but by our thinking. In other words, it's not what is going on in our lives that stops us from getting what we want, it's what we believe to be true that stops us. We are as happy as *we* have decided to be, or allowed ourselves to become but that will change as soon as we decide we deserve more.

We all deserve happiness. We all deserve peace and harmony. We all deserve love. But just as others cannot make us happy, they also cannot make us grow and keep moving. We are responsible for our own happiness and we are responsible for our own lives.

Yes, it is scary, but once we understand that our quality of life depends fully on who we are, what we *do* and the choices we make, then we can stop blaming others and take full responsibility for our lives.

Everything that we want to achieve in life and in our relationships is outside of our comfort zone.

I will talk about this later on in the book but in brief, if we want what we don't have, we have to do what we haven't done.

For example, if we are feeling left out and alone, and upset because we feel we have no friends, we can do a number of things, good and not so good. We can sit at home in our bedrooms feeling sorry for ourselves making up stories in our minds about why nobody likes us; we can choose to get upset and then take out our bad mood on our family; we can use this time to talk to a parent or loved one to express our feelings; we can distract ourselves from our feelings through mindless gaming; we can scroll through social media and feel worse about ourselves as we see others having a great time. There are numerous options, but here's a thought, we could actually leave the house and visit someone. We could call a friend up and say, "I could do with some company, fancy going for a walk or doing something together?"

Which choices are the easy ones? Which are the ones that scare us? It's the scary steps that we take that actually get us to where we want to be. If that was not the case, then we would already have everything that we want.

We go about our daily lives without stretching ourselves too much regardless of whether we are happy or not. But when we take a step outside of our comfort area, that is where we see and feel the best in ourselves. Now I'm not talking about doing scary things like bungee jumping off a bridge, I'm talking about stretching ourselves beyond our comfort levels, beyond our life skills and beyond our current abilities, to get better, and be better every day.

Imagine an individual that loves the theatre and wants to become an actor but they are too afraid to join the drama club or theatre group in case they are no good at it. How can they ever realise their dream if they don't even try? How will they ever truly know if they are any good, or if they even like acting? The only way to know is to push themselves to do something they are scared of. When we take those steps outside our circle of comfort and knowledge, we step into the unknown and take a chance on ourselves.

If we fall, we fall. We may fail but to me, the only real failure in life is never trying. Fear is the biggest killer of dreams, not lack of skill, ability, looks or person-ality…fear. But having the courage to go for what you want, or ask for what you want, is never a failure and always a win!

Stepping outside our comfort zone is where the magic happens and we feel like we can achieve all our goals and dreams. This does not mean that we have to feel uncomfortable and do what others want us to do, doing things that we don't want to, it means we have to follow our hearts and have the courage to step forward and claim our lives by ourselves, for ourselves.

Courage is not an absence of fear, it's coming face to face with our doubts and fears and wrestling with them head-on. When we do so, we take control of our lives and our destiny and realise that *we* have the power over our lives. We realise that we can be and do whatever we choose in life and we *can* overcome our fears and live life courageously.

When we step into our light, we reveal our self-worth and power.

In conclusion, being who we are and following our hearts by being our true and better selves, instead of doing what others are doing, is the path to self-love.

Am I Worth It?

As we are working our way through this book, we will become more and more clear about the people we are, why we are here and what makes a happy and fulfilling life. I'm not here to tell you what is right or wrong or to give you the answers but to help you by asking the right questions. You are the author of your life and you have to write your own story.

1. On a scale of 1–10 how much do I love myself at the moment? (1 being – I feel I am of no worth and find it hard to like myself, 10 being – I love the person I am or working to become).

2. How would I feel, act and behave if I was at a level 10 on the scale?

3. On a scale of 1–10, how loving am I…

    a.   To others?
    b.   To myself? (1 being I know I should be more loving but I'm not at all, 10 being I do all in my power to be the loving human being I know I am)

4. At what level on the scale would I like to be and why?

5. If I was to describe the way I look in detail to someone that has never met me so they would recognise me, how would I describe myself? (Include body shape, style, skin etc.)

6. If I have children in the future, what body part or feature would I hope they get from me and why?

7. What three character attributes would I like them to inherit from me and why?

a.
b.
c.

8. If I could clone myself and make three personality adjustments that would make me a better version of me, what good qualities would I add or improve?

a.
b.
c.

9. What three things can I do, or start working on now, to make a better version of me? For example: read books to help me to learn how to improve my life, make a lifestyle change, spend more time lifting others.

a.
b.
c.

10. I deserve to be loved, not only by others, but by me also because I am… (List all the things that make you an awesome human being)

11. Describe what an ideal best friend should be like. How should they treat me and others?

12. Am I being my own best friend? Do I think good thoughts and speak kindly about myself? If not, why not?

13. From today on, I will talk to myself using only kind and positive words because I am of great value, inside and out. I commit to being my own best friend because when I love who I am, I will feel... (Explain how you will feel when you become your own best friend).

I commit to being my best friend because...

Love Lesson #3
My Heart

"A loving heart is a powerful force in the world."

There are only a handful of things that any of us truly desire in life and the most precious one of all is love. We live for love. To love others and to be loved. When we have love in our hearts, we feel truly alive and can feel pure joy. No amount of fame, fortune, power, good looks or even good health matches the power of love.

Love, along with kindness and connection is the very essence of life and the reason we are here. We are here to support and love each other as we grow through life together, learning the lessons that we need to learn to shape us into who we need to be.

No person truly knows why we are here upon the earth and therefore we all have to live by faith. Faith that life will be beautiful and full of love, kindness and connection. Perhaps some believe the opposite, but whatever we *believe* to be true, *will* be true for us.

One truth is that we reap what we sow in life, which means we harvest what we plant. For example, if we plant pumpkin seeds in the ground, we harvest pumpkins. If we plant sunflower seeds, we grow sunflowers and so on. So, if we plant seeds of love and gratitude in our hearts, we will grow a heart full of love and gratitude. If we plant seeds of anger and resentment, or jealousy and hatred, that is exactly what we will reap. It really is that simple.

It's highly unlikely that we will grow sunflowers if we plant pumpkin seeds. Therefore, whatever we want, we have to plant the right seeds and nurture them. If we want love, joy, happiness and all good things in life, *we* have to plant the right seeds, take care of them and nourish them each day. If we want *love* but sow seeds of hatred and resentment in our hearts, guess what we will harvest? The more love we sow, the more we will reap but we also have to protect our seeds as they grow.

One of the main dangers that could stop plants from growing are weeds. They not only suck the energy and nutrients from the ground, but they can also literally wrap themselves around the plant and squeeze the life out of them.

We too have to watch out for life's weeds and remove them before they drain the life out of us as well. When we are small children it's our parents' job to keep us safe by ensuring that we are not exposed to them, but as we grow, we have to learn how to recognise the dangers for ourselves.

When we do learn how to recognise life's weeds and the threat they pose to our well-being, we can take the necessary steps to remove them to keep ourselves out of danger allowing us to be free to grow into the wonderful beings we were intended to be.

What are life's weeds? What are the dangers that can damage our growth and make it difficult for us to live and grow freely?

Some weeds come disguised as pretty flowers and because of that we can be reluctant to remove them but we have to listen to our hearts, tune out the opinions of the world and pluck out these sabotaging threats. If we don't remove them, we are putting our lives, health, happiness and well-being at risk.

Weeds show up in all shapes and sizes and have lots of disguises. One example is negative self-talk. It can start off with a negative comment such as: I'm so stupid or I'm so ugly but if we don't pluck out these weeds/negative thoughts as soon as we recognise them as weeds, we are allowing them to grow alongside us until they grab hold of us, wrap themselves around our hearts and slowly suck the life out of our self-worth. Another thing we have to watch out for is our own curiosity. I never really gave much thought to the old saying 'Curiosity killed the cat' but as I wrote this, I realised how significant it is to life.

It is only natural for young men and women, and human beings in general, to be curious, to want to know and experience life, but if we decide to go into unknown grounds, we need to be sure it is safe for us to enter. Let's not go into life's situations like a cat (without thinking it through properly) and get ourselves killed.

How do we decide if it is safe for us? By having a clear understanding of who we are and by living by our own guiding principles. They are our own personal guide in all aspects of life that we have written and created for ourselves to keep us safe and to remind us who we truly desire to be.

Instinctively we know what is right and what is wrong according to our own life rules, so whenever we are faced with a decision of whether to enter through a door to have a look, we have to be prepared to live with the consequences of what we see and experience.

For example, if all our friends are taking drugs and we too are curious to experience the effects of them, we should really ask ourselves:

- Do I *really* want to know?
- Why do I want to know?
- Would I be showing myself love by doing this?
- What are the dangers?

- What are the benefits, and what will I gain?
- Would I be doing it to impress others and to fit in?
- Am I ready to accept this responsibility regardless of any unwelcome consequences?
- Will this improve my life long term?
- What if I have a reaction to them?
- Will it take me on the road that I want to be on, or lead me away from it?
- How will it affect those I love, and those that love me?
- Do I have full control of the effects on my body?
- Will this bring me peace of heart long term?
- Is it worth the risk?
- How will it affect my future if I get caught doing something illegal?
- Am I listening to my heart or being influenced by the world?

Sometimes we get caught up in the moment and make split decisions but that is very unwise and can lead us away from who we are, and away from the peace and harmony inside of us.

If the people around us are using drugs, and encourage us, or talk us into doing it too, what does it say about them? Are they our true friends? What does that say about us? Are we so weak that we are willing to go against our own true self and follow others instead of our own heart?

True freedom comes from living a life following our heart and soul, being ourselves and spending our lives doing what we truly love with who we truly love. Captivity is the prison that we put ourselves in by listening to the world.

Okay, not everyone that has ever taken drugs has come into dire circumstances but how many success stories have you heard of about people taking recreational drugs? The only ones we hear of are from those that have overcome addictions to them, true? These people were led away from what they truly wanted. They did not love themselves or value themselves enough to put their hearts first. I can't imagine anyone on this entire planet having a dream of becoming a drug addict, can you? If they do exist, they are very much in need of some love.

Understanding who we are and what we want to plant in our lives and in our hearts, is essential. We are the artists of our own life and destiny, and we can choose to create a masterpiece or spend our whole lives expecting the picture to paint itself. 'Free will' is a blessing that we all have and we can choose to create, or break, an incredible world for ourselves.

We may have made mistakes in the past but we can always press the reset button and start to change today. It is never too late to start treating ourselves with the love we all deserve.

We could say there are two types of people in life. We are either flowers (let's say sunflowers again), or weeds. *We* have the power to decide which one we want to be.

Like a sunflower, we can grow tall and strong, radiate confidence, goodness and beauty. We also produce more good seeds which can be used to nourish the people of the world. Our good seeds fall around us and produce more sunflowers making this world a more colourful and beautiful place to be. Alternatively, we can choose to be a weed. We may even be a beautiful weed but we suck and squeeze the life out of others nearby. Is that how we want to be remembered?

The beauty of being a human being is that it does not matter which plant we originated from or what our backgrounds are, we have all been blessed with a choice of which character we want to play in life.

Because we are all born into this world as perfect human beings with a pure and perfect soul, we get to choose who we are. It's the choices that we make that determines who we want to become and also the quality of our lives. Do you want to grow tall and radiate strength, colour and beauty or do you want to suck the life out of those that surround you? What and whom do you choose to be?

In schools, we are taught that with hard work and study, we can *do* what we want to for a living, but we are not often (if ever at all) taught that we can also *be* whoever we want to be in life. We each have all the tools to create our own incredible masterpiece and design it exactly how we want it to be, but first, we need to have a vision. And where do we find this vision? Listening to your heart is the best place to start.

I Pledge to Live According to My Heart

Before we take a single step forward, we have to make a pledge, to make a commitment to ourselves, to continually work on becoming our best and true selves so that we know in advance what we desire to feel in our lives. To honour our true selves and our hearts.

My pledge to myself would look something like this: I pledge to always be true to my heart and to feel at peace with myself and with my life choices. To know that I am giving myself the best chance at living a happy and successful life through the choices that I make. I will not allow anything or anyone to lead me away from being the best version of myself to fulfil my life's purpose. The way I treat myself and my body is a reflection of how I deserve to be treated therefore I commit to treating myself with love in all areas of my life.

Now write your own personal pledge as a commitment to yourself:

I pledge to…

I AM 'THE ONE' AND THE CREATOR OF MY HAPPINESS AND DESTINY!

As I mention often, self-love and self-worth are essential to living a happy life. Not in a narcissistic kind of way or to be selfish and only think of ourselves, but to understand our inherent worth in order to create the relationships and lives that we desire.

We all have what it takes to create the lives that we deserve but unless we value our hearts, minds, bodies and souls, and love who we are, we will not realise how much power we truly have over our lives and our happiness. *We* create our happiness and no one other than ourselves can possess this power over us.

Most of us spend our lives looking for 'The One' to make us happy but 'The One' that we are actually searching for is *us*. The complete and wholehearted better versions of ourselves. We have to love our selves wholly, be grateful for all that we are and accept ourselves for who we are to feel complete. Only then are we truly ready to build a strong and long-lasting relationship.

'The One' we spend our lives looking for, is literally right under our noses. Once we realise that *we* are 'The One', we can go through life with all that we need to create an abundant life full of all that we desire, including a partner to spend our lives with.

Perhaps when we feel that lack of love, that empty space inside our hearts, we will look for others to fill it for us to make us feel whole, but again it is not their responsibility, it is ours.

If we feel insecure, we may subconsciously seek attention and love wherever we can find it, but in our desperation, we often look in the wrong places and are led down roads that we did not want to take. All because we felt we were not worth more.

Once we know our worth, we will not compromise or drop our standards. We stay in alignment with our guiding principles and we will know we deserve love from the right people who will treat us with the love and respect we deserve.

Some of us use our pets or other people (often the wrong people) to fill that empty space, to give us that sense of love and connection, and to make us feel wanted. Some use food, alcohol or drugs. Some use gambling, social media and gaming, but these temporary distractions steer us away from looking within ourselves and the essential work of learning to love and value who we were born to be.

So why do we avoid looking within? Do we even know who we are? Have we ever asked ourselves questions such as:

"Do I like myself? If not, why not? What kind of human being am I? What kind of human being do I want to be? If I had someone like me in my life, how would I feel? Do I appreciate who I am? What are my good qualities? What positive attributes do I possess to offer the world?"

Or do we just struggle on feeling worth less than others, believing that we will just have to make do with less than what we truly want?

Why do we use all these distractions to hide behind? I believe it is fear. Fear of facing the reality of life, fear of rejection and failure, and fear of living a life being unloved and insignificant. There is one thing I fear more than anything in life, and that is regret. To imagine that I come to the end of my life, look back and wish I'd tried harder. To wish I'd opened my heart more and built strong and loving relationships. I am a naturally shy person but I step out of my comfort zone to make conversations with people all the time because I love meeting people. If I waited for people to come into my life, I would have missed out on all the wonderful people that have crossed my path.

We go through life investing in material items such as cars or the latest electronic devices to feel we are living an abundant lifestyle but how much time do we invest into meeting new people and building new relationships? How much do we open ourselves to love? When we are small, we make friends easily because we have no insecurities and have nothing to fear. But as we get older, sometimes we begin to doubt ourselves and worry if we will fit in or even be liked at all. We hold ourselves back and don't open up to people, but my philosophy is that if we keep the doors of our hearts closed, how can anyone enter?

Like all things in life, it is better to try and fail than to live in fear of failure of not being liked or accepted. As I say always, the only real failure in life is never trying, whether that is in our relationships, in our work, in our studies or in our life's purpose. If we consistently act on fulfilling our dreams and fail, we can rest knowing that we gave it our everything.

As children when we want some love, we cuddle whoever we please and literally throw ourselves into the arms of everyone we want a hug from, but as we get older, we begin to stop and wonder whether we should or not. We fear rejection. Especially as the world is today, everyone is so busy with life and the fast-paced life of living that people barely have time just to be still. People no longer get bored and have time to just stop and think about how we can make others smile. We no longer just pop round to friends for a cuppa and a chat, we message them. When we need some love and connection, we feel we have to plan in advance, disturb someone, or take them away from what they are doing, so we hold ourselves back and distract ourselves in other ways.

The generations gone by didn't have the problems that we face today because they didn't have affluent lives like we have. We practically have everything we need at the touch of a button.

For example, if we are hungry, we don't need to gather the food and prepare it before we eat it. We don't need to milk the cow to get some milk, we just nip to the shop or open the fridge.

The people were not comparing themselves to others, only striving to love and provide for their families. They were happy with what they had and were grateful for the simple things in life. For food, water, a warm and safe home, for their families and their faith. They got their exercise by being outside working on growing their own foods, hunting and gathering. They often made their own clothes washed them by hand and they walked almost everywhere. They took care of their families and communities but they were content and grateful for all that they had.

They weren't competing in a fast-paced world clambering to the top of the ladder pushing others out of the way as they go. The women didn't value themselves on how they looked because they were busy focusing on taking care of their families. Men didn't value themselves by their job title or what kind of car they drove, they were focused on providing for their families. Now times have changed and responsibilities are shared in life, but none of us seem clear on which roles we should play anymore. We spend more time working so we can buy more things to keep up with this material world but is that filling our hearts, or just our pockets, bellies and homes?

These days we tend to measure ourselves by what we look like, what we do for a living, our material possessions and the like, but we can be left empty inside. We seek to be accepted by society's standards without taking the time to know ourselves and know what we truly want. It is then that we begin to feel less than others, or worse still, better than others. When it's every man for himself and we fight to win the race of life, we forget about those that are left behind. To be truly happy and to live a successful life we have to be living a purpose-filled life, to move forward holding hands with those within our reach to lead the way, not run ahead without any thought for others.

The old saying 'We rise by lifting others' means that when we love, support and help others in life we ourselves are lifted in heart and spirit, and feel that sense of worth within our hearts.

When we compare ourselves to others and don't match up to them, we feel less than worthy. We seek out things to give us a lift to make us feel content or give us that rush but the feeling never lasts. We value ourselves by how many 'likes' we get on social media not by who we truly are as human beings. We feel lifted by getting 'likes' and feel worthless when we get little reaction, but is this real life? Is it allowing us to live our life's purpose? Instead of taking time to lift others, we often put on a show to the world of what we think will make us popular or get attention, but are we showcasing our bodies and faces, or revealing our true selves from our heart and soul?

Once we start being our true 'heart' selves and living by our guiding principles, we will always be able to create happiness in life.

As soon as we stop comparing ourselves with others and start comparing ourselves with the person we desire to become, we can make the necessary changes to take us to where we need to go. As we do so, our lives will begin to improve and our hearts will begin to fill with love for ourselves and others.

As a teenager, I felt a lack of love for myself because I compared myself to others. I had created a picture of myself in my own head using the opinions of others instead of looking into my heart to see who I was.

Isn't it funny how we always focus on all the unkind things people say about us but when people say nice things, we find it hard to accept the compliment? Ten people can say how lovely we are but if one says we are not, we believe it to be true. *We* give their unkind words value. Their words are of no value unless *we* pay attention to them and bring them to life. But if we loved who we are, we would not care what others say.

I hated being by myself because I didn't like my own company. I needed to be surrounded by other people, if not I would feel empty. The picture I had created of myself in my head was that I was: not pretty enough, not good enough, not worthy enough and not clever enough, so I was always looking for others to fill that emptiness within my heart. Somehow having boyfriends made me feel significant but I still didn't feel of any true value. The one thing I did have though was a determined and fighting spirit that nobody could break. I used to tell myself that one day I was going to be a somebody. Not be a nobody.

I carried the feeling of being unloved as a small child into my teenage years as I had never expressed my feelings to my mum or dealt with my feelings. If only I had been brave enough then to open up to her, I know she would have helped me to deal with my feelings, but I was scared she would be upset with me and I feared more rejection.

I don't remember doing it purposefully but before the age of seven, I refused to eat family meals and caused my poor mum a lot of distress. I would hear the clanging of the plates in the kitchen at mealtimes and that was my cue to lock myself in the bathroom. I must have driven my mum crazy. As a mother now, I realise how frustrating that would have been for her, but I just didn't want to eat, and my mum would get so angry with me.

She used to call the doctor in every week to check on me but he was not worried and used to say: "When she's hungry enough, she'll eat," but Mum made the mistake of allowing me to eat ice cream and crisps so of course, I was never hungry.

The battle between me and my mum went on for years. Me fighting for attention and her fighting to keep me nourished. Neither of us were purposely hurting each other but both of us felt unloved and were in pain.

As I look back and analyse my childhood, I can see why I felt the way I did. My big sister Marisa was a model child and did as she was told without question and then I arrived. A fiery child with a strong spirit that questioned *everything* (which I inherited from my mum). My mum was quite rightfully proud of my sister but I most probably felt like I was a disappointment. Marisa was an angel and I was not, to say the least, especially when my little sister arrived. Marisa and I still laugh about our childhood characters as neither of us have changed that much. She still does as she is told to please everyone and I still question everything with my determined spirit, and I fight for what's right.

Two months after I was born, my mum got pregnant with my little sister Gisella, and because I never really had that one to one time with my mum, I suffered. Mum used to tell me stories of how I used to harm my poor little sister. We used to laugh about it but I can imagine how naughty I must have been.

On one occasion I pulled my tiny baby sister off the couch where my mum had safely left her (well so she thought) and she fell with a thump, to which Marisa and I found pretty funny. When we were a little bigger, I gave Gisella a candleholder (the ones you put in birthday cakes), told her it was a 'sweetie' and told her to eat it, which she did. Thankfully my mum managed to put her fingers down poor Gisella's throat to pull it out but it did scratch her throat pretty badly.

I have no recollection of these incidents because I was so small but no doubt I would have been punished for my antics and most likely told that I was a bad girl, and in those days received a good smack. I grew up believing that I was not a good girl and therefore not loved.

As I got older, I realised why I felt like I did, why I behaved the way I did, and why I felt I was never good enough. All I wanted was love. That is all any of us really want, isn't it…? To be loved.

As a teenager, I believed self-love was a bad thing. It was an insult if we were told that we loved ourselves. We would even defend ourselves and say 'I do not love myself!'. It's funny really. In fact, I would even judge others and say things like: "I don't like them, they love themselves!"

I would dress down at times so I could just blend in and not be noticed. I would try not to stand out just in case people thought I loved myself. At other times I went on rebellious streaks and wore some outrageous head-turning outfits (most likely to get the love and attention that I craved). I didn't even like the clothes that I was wearing but I wanted to be on-trend and fit in with society.

I remember at 16 saying to my friends, "I can't wait to be forty because then I can wear beautiful dresses and high heels." That was who I was then but I was wearing hoodies and flats, or the fashionable leather skirts with fishnet tights (well it was the eighties).

That was the fashion and I wanted to be accepted. I was conforming to the world and to what others were doing even though in my heart and mind I was elegantly walking around in a beautiful dress and heels. I was so far from being the real me, which resulted in me not really liking myself.

I wasn't listening to my heart but listening to the world. I was reacting to my lack of self-love and worth instead of looking to resolve it. They didn't teach self-love at school and at the time, I didn't think it was a problem and continued to search for 'the one' to fill my heart.

And then my knight in shining armour came into my life and saved me.

Not long before my 16th birthday, I met the love of my life (well so I thought at the time). He was an amazing guy who made me laugh and I finally felt truly loved. I felt I belonged to him and he was mine forever. My family loved him and he became my mum and dad's fourth child and I finally found what I was looking for. I fell head-over-heels in love with him and thought he was 'The One' I wanted to spend my life with.

But…he was a teenage boy. And teenage boys want to be out enjoying life and having fun but I wanted him to be with me. When he was out without me, I was sitting at home crying. He would say he'd pick me up at 7 pm and I'd be sitting ready to go out and he'd turn up at 11 pm. Being in love just wasn't what I thought it would be but I put up with it because I loved him. After a couple of years, he settled down and my life was good and I was really happy. The problem was that my happiness all depended on how he treated me. When he was treating me well and I was the centre of his attention I was happy, but when he was doing his own thing and living his own life, which was his right as a human being, I felt like he didn't love me. I felt as though he would rather be with his friends than with me which I thought made me not as good as them. I was so insecure within myself and all I craved was love. He even confessed that he had cheated on me a couple of times but I forgave him. I felt like I was of no worth but I loved him, so I accepted it. Most of the time, we were happy and he made me laugh a lot. He was quite the joker which I loved until the joke was on me.

I was 19 and it was Christmas Day. We were all sat around the living room opening our presents and he handed me this tiny box. He and my sister were grinning from ear to ear sitting forwards in anticipation of my reaction. I couldn't help but smile as I unwrapped my gift. My heart began to race in excitement. Is it what I hoped it would be?

I slowly opened the box and there was a diamond chip ring looking back at me with a tiny receipt with the words 'engagement ring' written on it and my heart leapt for joy. My prayers had been answered.

I looked up to see my sister and my boyfriend rolling around the floor laughing at me and my reaction. "JOKE!" they both shouted. "You should have seen your face!" they said laughing. I forced a laugh and pretended that I got the joke but it was not funny at all. How could they think this was funny? Did they even know who I was? If they knew me at all, they would have known how much this would have hurt me.

My heart was truly broken and all my dreams were shattered as I realised that this was not the man for me. I made a vow to myself that I would never allow myself to be hurt by him again. We stayed together for another 4 years after that but things were never the same. I loved him and remained faithful to him but I knew that I would never marry him or spend my whole life with him. He became like a brother and that's how it stayed. I didn't end our relationship because he and everyone else were happy with our relationship, even if I wasn't, but I didn't want to hurt anyone. After all, he didn't mean to break my heart, he didn't even know at the time.

I didn't want to be with anyone else because in my mind, he had been the one. I couldn't even imagine a life without him so I kept my pain inside and carried on as if nothing was wrong but I was deeply unhappy, a feeling I was very used to.

But the good thing that came out of 'The Joke' was a determination to live my life for me and not for anyone else. I believed then that I had no control over my love life but I had control over my work life and put all my love into my work. My broken heart fuelled me. The salon I was managing became my life and due to my enthusiasm for my work, I was building a great name for myself and was earning really good money.

I began living my life for myself. I started going out with my girlfriends and we'd have so much fun. Dancing allowed me to feel free to be me and was my escape from my inner pain. I never drank very much alcohol as I didn't like it much, or the feeling of being out of control and I didn't need it to have fun, in fact it just spoiled the fun. The times that I did drink a lot I ended up feeling and looking dreadful at the end of the night which put me off.

So, my broken heart turned out to be the best thing for me. It woke me up to another part of me and I began to gain some self-worth especially in my ability to use my gifts and talents. I had previously put so much of myself into my relationship that I had neglected me and my dreams but not anymore.

Everything that happens to us, good and bad, is for our own good, even if we don't believe it at the time or understand it. Life happens for us, not against us, meaning that everything that we go through is to lead us to where we need to be, to live our happiest lives and fulfil our purpose, not to hurt us or to punish us.

Once we understand this, we can look for opportunities to learn and grow from every situation in life, even when we feel broken and helpless.

In the four years that I remained in this relationship, I even opened my own salon with a friend. My ex-boss was selling up and we were told we were going to lose our jobs but instead of feeling like a victim, I used this opportunity to challenge myself and to grow. I had a chance to start my own business at 21 years old and I took it. Yes, I was scared. Yes, I was taking a risk. But I was taking a risk on myself and I knew I could do it but I had to act, not just believe and hope, and I did it. We built a thriving business.

If that engagement ring would have been real, all the passion and ambition would have been wasted along with my gifts and talents. Instead of allowing my broken heart to destroy me, I used it to make me. I began to realise the power I had over my own life and this was my first big step to realising my strength and worth as a human being.

When I did finally end my relationship after almost eight years together it was hard. It was one of the hardest things I have ever had to do. I had to put myself before another human being which was not in my nature but I had a choice. I had to ask myself:

'Do I want to marry this man and spend the rest of my life with him or am I going to set him free to be loved the way he deserves to be loved? Am I willing to sacrifice my happiness for his? Am I brave enough to face the devastation that will follow?'

My new-found self-worth had made my boyfriend uneasy and I could sense his fear of losing me, but the reality was that he had lost me many years before between the cheating and the joke. I no longer loved him in that way, but I still loved him like my brother and our families were really close so I wasn't just breaking his heart, I was breaking up a family.

I hated myself for doing it but I loved myself enough to know that we both deserved more. While he was still with me, he was not able to find a new love so not breaking up with him would be worse. We all deserve love.

I did consider staying with him just to keep the peace and make him happy but I asked myself:

"Would I be happy if someone stayed with me because they *had* to? Would I want someone to feel trapped in a relationship with me even if they didn't love me?"

Of course, I wouldn't want that, so I decided to face my fear and do what needed to be done. I ended our relationship and I broke his heart.

The devastation that followed was worse than I'd imagined. Everyone hated me and my own mother refused to speak to me for two weeks after asking, "How could you do this to me?" It was really hard to be the horrible person that destroyed so many lives, but in my heart, I knew it was the best thing and so I took all the abuse, I understood their pain. I learned a lot about being the bad one that ends a relationship. People attack you, call you names and blame you for all the destruction but nobody tries to understand you. I was in tremendous pain too but nobody asked me if I was Okay. Nobody cared if I did the right thing or not, all they could see was an evil and selfish act. I was also losing a brother that I loved and it wasn't easy for me to see him in pain and not be able to help him. I was setting him free but it was heartbreaking for me also. In time we all moved on but I still had to carry the guilt around with me which was my price to pay, but I deserved to be happy too.

This experience taught me a lot about life. At times we need to make difficult choices that others may not like or agree with but we cannot live our lives to make others happy. We are all responsible for our own happiness.

It also made me realise that people that end relationships are not always bad people even though they are looked upon as evil. I wasn't married with children and I had made no commitment therefore I had a choice of whether to stay in an unhappy relationship or go, so I chose my happiness. Yes, I was scared. I asked myself whether I would ever find anyone that would love me again but I knew in my heart that I would rather be alone, or spend my life searching for my soul mate, instead of just making do or being less than happy. When we listen to our inner soul, our true selves, we actually know when something is not right but we often try to ignore our intuition (our gut feeling) because we don't really want to face the truth.

We owe it to ourselves to live our lives being true to our hearts and to make the right decisions no matter how hard it may seem. We have to trust our inner voice and choose what is right. We have to let go of people and things that we know don't allow us to be the best versions of us or else it will bring us down and ultimately destroy us or imprison us in a life we did not want.

We are here on this earth to learn and experience life, and everything that happens, happens for a reason but we have a choice whether to learn and grow from it or whether to lay down and be a victim. We love and are loved yet we are often hurt. We give and are given in life yet we often lose. These are all life's lessons from which we can learn but ultimately, we choose our own destiny. We can play the cards we are dealt in life or we can just sit back and watch others play the game for us. The choice is entirely ours.

As long as we treat all people with love and kindness and always do the right thing, we can live in peace with ourselves and with our life choices.

I share my experiences and stories, and what I learned from them to help others; for them to learn from too. Due to our lack of experience in our teens we only have the advice of our peers to go on as we rarely talk to our parents or other adults about our personal stuff. Well I certainly didn't and even if I would have gotten advice from my parents, I doubt I would have listened.

Times change but the essence of life and love stay the same. Our hearts feel the same and love is love in any era. What we see in the movies, in magazines, on social media and the like isn't real life and all of us know it. We don't post selfies or videos of ourselves on social media having disagreements with our loved ones. We don't post when we feel less than perfect, we post the best pictures and sometimes even edit them to make ourselves look better than we really are. True? So, we cannot compare ourselves or our relationships with others.

Before we go into a relationship, we first need to decide what we want and what kind of relationship we are looking for. Are we looking for someone to fill an emptiness within us or to hold our hands and be a support and comfort to us? Do we need someone to tell us how wonderful and beautiful we are to help us to feel of worth or do we understand our true value? Do we love ourselves sufficiently to know what we deserve in a partner or in our lives?

We don't always ask ourselves the right questions before making life decisions or before getting into relationships because we get swept up in the moment of being desired or wanted, which makes us feel significant, but it's important for us to decide beforehand how we want to be treated and what kind of person we want to share our lives with.

We all deserve to be treated with love and respect, and treated the way we want to be treated, but what are our standards? How do we want to be treated? I see young people getting into relationships that are not really what they want because they fear having no one, so they accept less than they deserve, but ultimately it will lead them to unhappiness, unless they decide they are worth more.

Some partners are very controlling and possessive over us and we may confuse that with feeling loved. We may think that they really love us because they don't want to ever be apart from us, or they ask us not to go out with our friends because they want to spend time with us, but that is their insecurity, not their love.

Whether it is our partners or us ourselves that are being possessive, things have to change in order for us to have a healthy and happy relationship. We may not do it purposefully or realise that we are even doing it, and it does not mean we are bad people, it means we are just fearful of losing what we have and hang on too tightly because of our insecurities.

If our partners truly love us, they will allow us to keep being who we are and not change us into who they want us to be and vice versa. People don't belong to us, and if we try to cage them in, they will naturally feel unhappy and want to be free even if they love us. Personally, I want someone to be by my side because they want to be there, not because they feel they have to be. After being cheated on I made a choice to always be honest with whoever I am with. It is one of my guiding principles to treat others as I wish to be treated. If someone does not want to be with me anymore, I want to know. I only agreed to marry my husband after he promised that he would tell me if he stopped loving me or no longer wanted me in his life. I believe that if we truly love someone, we will set them free and allow them to love whoever their heart truly desires. For me, honesty is always the best policy even if I am hurt. It's always better to know the truth. Yes, the truth may hurt but the alternative is far worse. If we don't know something is wrong, how can we try to mend it or make it right?

If we are not being treated with the love and kindness that we deserve, we are saying that this is acceptable to us. If we change who we truly are to be who others want us to be, we begin to lose our own identities and lose a part of ourselves which prevents us from being free to just be. We may change to make others happy but we are being unfair to ourselves and are preventing our own personal growth, which is the very essence of life: to love, to learn and to *grow*. So, before we promise to love another, we should first make a promise to ourselves.

My Personal Promise

I promise myself to allow only kind, loving and honest people into my heart who are willing to grow with me and love me for who I really am. To respect me in all that I choose to do and support me in becoming the very best version of me. I promise to treat others as I wish to be treated and to be open and honest in all my relationships so that I will be treated in the same way. I understand that I reap what I sow so I will plant seeds of love and goodness wherever I go in order to receive the same. I promise to listen to my innermost self and always choose the right path that will lead me to a peaceful, happy and fulfilling life.

This is part of a promise I have made in my heart to myself to remind me of my worth and how I deserve to be treated. It is essential to decide beforehand how we want to be treated by others and to set ourselves an acceptable standard. Writing our own personal promise means that we know how we deserve to be treated and will not accept anything less. Now it's your turn.

I promise myself…

Answering the following questions will not only help you to decide the kind of people you want to allow into your heart, but also to allow you to recognise them when you see them.

We tend to be attracted to people by the way they look but it is equally important that we love them for their soul, their hearts and their minds. In time, looks will fade but their beautiful souls will always remain.

1. What ten personality traits are essential in a future life partner, and why they are important to me? (Use the list as a guide.)

Kind	Trustworthy	Sensible
Loving	Wise	Charismatic
Thoughtful	Ambitious	Strong
Cheerful	Caring	Motivated
Faithful	Enthusiastic	Forgiving
Positive	Passionate	Outgoing
Funny	Patient	Humble
Warm	Generous	Quiet
Friendly	Affectionate	Supportive
Sensitive	Honest	Understanding
	Responsible	Compassionate

a.

b.

c.

d.

e.

f.

g.

h.

i.

j.

2. Describe a perfect date with the partner of your dreams. Without using past experiences to influence your thoughts, what you would do, where you would go, how you would feel, what would you talk about?

For example: A perfect date would be a walk on the beach holding hands while we walk and talk. We talk about our dreams and aspirations and how we are going to achieve them. I feel free to be myself and free to speak from my heart without fear of being judged. We stop for a healthy smoothie or gelato and enjoy the peaceful sea view. We are comfortable just sitting in silence as we listen to the water splashing against the rocks. I feel at peace with myself and am fully living in this moment.

Now it's your turn.

A perfect date would be…

3. Describe your ideal partner in detail: what their interests are; what kind of music they listen to; what kind of movies they watch; and what their passions are.

4. Even though other people cannot make us happy or make us feel any form of emotion, describe how you feel when you are with your ideal partner, (again not using any past experiences to influence your thoughts) making sure you do not say 'they make me feel'.

For example: When I am with my ideal partner, I feel happy, safe and loved. I feel safe being my true self and free to be me. I feel powerful, confident and strong in their presence yet protected.

When I am with my ideal partner, I feel…

5. Describe what your ideal future will look like with your ideal partner – marriage, children and lifestyle.

Sticks and Stones

"When we are in our twenties, we care what everyone thinks about us.

When we are in our forties, we don't care what anyone thinks of us.

When we are in our sixties, we realise that people were never thinking about us at all!"

When I read words similar to this for the first time, I was pretty pleased with myself that I reached this level of wisdom on my own, thankfully before reaching sixty, and I wanted to share this wisdom with you also.

PEOPLE DON'T REALLY CARE WHAT WE LOOK LIKE, HOW WE ACT OR WHAT WE DO! They may express their opinion of us but they don't really care. Those that love us will be by our side, hold our hands through life and help to guide us. Those that don't love us, couldn't care less about what we do or don't do. They may criticise us, judge us or try to put us down, but why care about what they think?

Being around uncaring people isn't necessarily a bad thing, it just means that they are minding their own business just as we are minding ours, and that we are actually not that interesting to them. Why would we be?

Think about when we look at a group photo that we know that we are in. The first thing we do is search for ourselves and how we look in the photo. Then we look for our friends and family but we don't inspect the rest of the people in the photo unless they mean something to us, whether it's in a positive or negative way. Unless we are a celebrity or public figure, people tend not to even notice.

I tested out this theory after I was set a challenge while reading the book 'Thank and Grow Rich' by Pam Grout. She challenged the readers to go out in a public place and lie down for just a few seconds to see what reaction we got from others.

I wasn't quite brave enough to do it on my own so my daughter Maia agreed to do it with me. We didn't tell anyone what we were planning and one busy Sunday afternoon when we were out for a walk with my sister and our families in a busy seaside town, Maia and I laid down in the middle of the square with more than 100 people surrounding us. We were a little scared but we did it anyway, and laid on the ground giggling away. A few people turned to look at us for a second but they just as quickly looked away. My husband and sister just rolled their eyes at us as if to say 'What are they up to now?' but they just kept on walking and talking. Maia and I jumped up after a few seconds astounded by the reaction… NO REACTION!

I learned a valuable lesson that day. I realised that worrying what others think of us is a complete waste of time and energy, that our fears are not real. People are too busy with their own lives to focus on or care about ours, and this experiment proved it.

A few weeks later when I was in town, I tripped up while crossing the road, not just a little stumble but a complete nosedive that stretched out over half of the pedestrian crossing. The cars stopped and four people came running to my rescue to help me up. Apart from my scraped knees and hands (and damaged pride), I escaped unharmed from my public spectacle. While I hobbled away, I realised that people care and notice when it really matters, even if we wished they hadn't.

I urge you to do this little experiment (not the nosedive) as it gave me a great sense of freedom, liberating me from the fear of what people are thinking. You have to experience it for yourself to really understand its profound effect. We spend half of our lives worrying about what others think of us but why does it even matter? How does it change or affect our lives? The only person's thoughts that we have to care about is our own. We have to spend every waking moment with 'Me, Myself and I' and our thoughts, so they are the only thoughts we should care about. The only unkind thoughts that can do us any harm are our own, so it is essential that we are kind and loving to ourselves.

If others do not value us, they either do not understand us, or do not know us. How they feel about us cannot affect us unless we allow it to. It is literally their problem if they have a problem with us.

As long as people are not physically harming us, words and opinions can do us no harm.

"Sticks and stones may break my bones but words can never hurt me!" is what my sisters and I used to say to ourselves as children being bullied for being of mixed race, and different to them.

It wasn't easy to ignore the verbal bullying but I knew the words of the rhyme were true. The more reaction people got from us the more they tormented us, so I just tried to ignore it. Because my little sister was always bigger than me, she used to try to protect me. If anyone said anything to upset us, she would react in anger and chase the other kids away but that just gave them more ammunition. When the bullies stopped getting a reaction they started to back off as it was no fun for them anymore. They lost their power.

If someone makes it quite clear that they don't like us, that is purely their decision and their right as a human being. We don't have to like *everyone* or be liked by everyone, but treating everyone with kindness no matter how unpleasant they are, gives *us* power and strength over our own actions and reactions, which allows us to rise above it.

If we are upset by others unkind words, it is because we are valuing their opinion and trusting them more than we trust ourselves. We are not who other people tell us we are, or what they think we are, it is purely their opinion, and their opinion of us belongs to them. They can think what they like about us… IT IS ACTUALLY NONE OF OUR BUSINESS! And nobody knows us better than we know ourselves.

We are each responsible for our own problems and if we have a problem with someone else's behaviour, dress sense or lifestyle, we have to work on ourselves. We cannot look into the heart and mind of others to see what they have been through, what they have had to endure in their lives; therefore, we cannot judge them.

We all make mistakes, every single one of us. Perhaps we lose our temper, say unkind things from time to time or make some extremely bad choices which lead us down a rocky road, so we have no right to judge others for their behaviour or the way they look. All we can do is keep an open heart and mind and be a good example and influence in our own lives.

Influence

We influence others through our words, behaviour and actions whether we want to or not. How we treat ourselves and others affects not only our lives, but the lives of those around us. This means we too are influenced by the people in our lives, so we have to be very aware of the behaviour of those we spend time with. Are we learning good habits from them or not-so-good?

In order for us to avoid taking on the undesirable habits and traits of others and choose a different way to be, we have to decide beforehand who we want to be and also who we choose to spend the majority of our time with. If we are surrounded by negative people who complain constantly yet do nothing to improve their lives, we can find ourselves falling into that same pattern.

For example, I don't like bad language, I never have. I just feel it is completely unnecessary and opens us up to negativity. Personally, I associate people swearing with anger, complaining or moaning because I have been on the receiving end of the energy of those words which I want to steer clear of. Because I have 'using good clean language' as one of my guiding principles, I am not influenced and will not pick it up from others. I believe swearing is a choice because we don't do it when we talk with our boss, teacher or parents which proves we have control over our words and our language. Words are so powerful and can make or break people so I like to choose them and use them wisely.

There are so many things in life that we don't have control of, like other people's actions and behaviour, but we have complete control over ourselves and our words, behaviour and actions so I choose to be a good influence. Doing so makes me feel at peace with myself and feel in alignment with my higher self.

My parents rarely swore (well not in English so I would understand) so therefore it didn't feel natural to me.

They did, however, both smoke cigarettes, and so did almost all of my friends, so it seemed natural for me to smoke too. I smoked for about five years of my life but I actually hated it.

I hated the smell and the taste but again I wanted to fit in and be like everyone else so stupidly persevered and ate mints while I smoked to disguise the taste and smell. I stopped smoking soon after I was diagnosed with asthma. Instead of listening to myself and my body, I had let myself be influenced by other's lifestyle choices which led me away from what I knew to be right for me.

Months after I stopped smoking, chronic asthma almost took my life on more than one occasion. I was paying the price for my bad choices in the past but again my struggle and near-death experiences were there to teach me something which took me on another journey. A journey back to good health. It was a long and difficult road but I never gave up because I wanted to live. My life and health were in my hands and I was determined to improve them both.

One of my favourite quotes ever by the late Henry Ford is:

"Whether you believe you can or you can't, you are right!"

This is such a powerful quote that I now live by and it has served me well. We all have the power to do what we want in this world but it's all down to what we *believe* we can do. I believed I would get my health back, and I did.

We have to listen to, and follow our hearts, and not be led by the world, or influenced by other people's actions. If I had believed that I would not get better, I would not have made the essential changes necessary to improve my life. I refused to accept mediocre health and a mediocre life. I wanted to live a healthy and energetic life, not endure a life where I couldn't walk up a flight of stairs without having to stop for breath. Nobody quite believed that I could turn my health around and reach my goal of being medication free but I did not let the negative people influence me and I kept believing and working on my goal.

The people around me criticised my new lifestyle choices as I refused all refined or processed food including sugar and alcohol, as well as dairy, cake and chocolate, but I got better, and eventually was healthier than I had ever been in my life.

Judging Others

None of us are perfect, we all make mistakes, and we are all guilty at times so we should also be more forgiving towards others as well as ourselves. No matter where we are in our lives at the moment, all it takes is a decision to change.

I had made mistakes but instead of hating myself or blaming God for my illness, I decided to do what needed to be done to improve the quality of my life. I took back control of my life instead of letting my life control me. I made a decision to improve, a decision to grow, and learn from it.

We all make mistakes so we cannot judge others for their life choices as we are not living their lives and have no idea how they are feeling, or why they choose to live the way they do.

In the Bible it says: "He that is without sin among you, let him cast a stone." But what does that mean?

I am by no means qualified to interpret the Bible but what the following story means to me is that unless we are perfect (which none of us are, even if we like to think we are), we cannot judge others, their lifestyle or their actions.

When Jesus was on the earth, there was a woman that had committed a sin. She was caught in the act of adultery, or prostitution, and dragged from her home into the street. The punishment for this crime in those days was a public stoning, which means the sinner stood while the public threw stones at them. Jesus was said to have been nearby while this was going on and when the people had stones in their hands ready to throw them at this woman, someone asked Jesus what they should do to this sinful woman, to which he answered: "He that is without sin among you, let him cast a stone at her." (In other words, whoever is perfect and has never made a mistake, they can throw a stone.)

Of course, none of us have ever been, nor ever will be, perfect and therefore none of us should be throwing any stones.

If Jesus didn't judge an adulterer/prostitute, should we?

We all make mistakes and because none of us are perfect, we too should put down the metaphorical stones that we have in our hands ready to throw. We cannot see into the hearts and minds of others and know the pain they feel or comprehend their reasoning, just as others can't look into our hearts and minds and understand us.

Once again, we need to treat others as we wish to be treated. If we don't want to be judged, we should not judge others. If we want to be treated with love and respect, we should treat others with love and respect. Yes, it really is that simple!

Love Through Service

"The joy of living comes through giving."

The more love we give unconditionally the more we receive. It is simply the law of the universe. We reap what we sow, we get what we give and when we serve others in our lives, we are gifted with a heart full of love and a deep contentment in life. Nothing compares to the long-lasting 'high' that we receive from lifting others. It not only gives our lives meaning, it actually creates happiness in the giver *and* the receiver. When we serve others, we realise our self-worth and also realise the power we have in making this world a little brighter.

At one point in my life after the death of my father and after my closest friend moved overseas, I got lost in the fog of my own thoughts and in the negativity surrounding me. I felt sad, lonely and helpless over my life but I was blessed with an opportunity to serve another human being that opened my heart again. I met Licia.

Licia was an old lady that lived across the road from me. She and her husband were in their 90s but they kept themselves to themselves, so other than a polite hello, I didn't really know them.

When I heard that her husband had died, I approached Licia one day and offered my condolences and asked her if I could do anything for her but she politely declined.

Then one day I saw her at the supermarket 5 km away and she was piling litres of soya milk into the basket of her three-wheeler bike so I ran over and insisted that I take her shopping home for her.

I could see that she was a little reluctant but I insisted as she already had a 5 km cycle ahead of her. I could only imagine how hard it would be for her to pedal if she had another six kilos of shopping to weigh her down. She was a tiny little lady and couldn't have weighed more than 40 kilos herself.

When she arrived home, she was grateful to have her shopping waiting for her and her face softened as she thanked me profoundly for my kindness.

From that moment on, we began to chat often while she was outside working on her garden, which she loved to do. My children loved climbing her trees to pick fruit for her, especially because they got to keep most of it. After all, she could only eat so much on her own.

We became great friends and from then on, I took her shopping in the car which turned out to be a weekly fun-filled social event for us.

Licia and I developed a deep friendship as I listened to the stories of her childhood and how things were so different to our present way of life. I loved spending time with her, and she with me. Her only son lived an hour away and only came to visit every few months as he himself was a pensioner so she only had me and another elderly neighbour to talk to.

My kids and I began spending every Sunday morning at her house playing cards and laughing together as she would accuse them of cheating. She became a part of our family in only a few short weeks and we all loved her dearly.

Within a few months however her health began to deteriorate and very soon she was housebound, had lost her appetite and had no desire to cook, so I began taking a plate of food over for her every day to encourage her to eat and she was so grateful. It was a joy to see her face light up every time I walked in the door.

As time went on, she began to feel low as she was no longer able to do work in her garden or get around easily. Her frail 91-year-old body was restricting her and it was making her unhappy.

One day the kids and I popped in to play cards but she just lay on the couch and said she wasn't up to it. I could see that she was low in spirit so I suggested that we play only one game and she accepted. That one game turned into an hour and we left her looking cheerful and bright again. We all came away feeling brighter as the children loved being around her and vice versa.

I felt truly blessed to be able to serve her and to give my children the opportunity to feel good about themselves in the service of others.

Licia gave me as much as I gave her though. As I had been feeling down myself before meeting her, she had unknowingly given me the love that I needed. Because both my parents had passed, I felt I was in need of some parental love which she gave me. Being around her and serving her led me to having a sense of worth again and a feeling that I was of value in this world. She brought so much meaning and a renewed energy to my life that I was deeply grateful for. We were both serving our purpose in our lives through giving and receiving love.

She died only a few weeks later but before she left, she thanked me for my friendship and said that in the 91 years that she had lived on the earth, she had never had a friend like me. She had never experienced so much love in a friend and said she wished she had met me earlier. From that moment on I realised that we each have the power to touch the hearts of our fellow human beings to bring them joy to their lives, even if only for a short time.

I began to see that I was of more worth than I had realised, and that I mattered. Each and every one of us have the power of love in our hands, to give and receive but it is entirely up to us if we use this gift or waste it. When we use it, we can create joy in the world and in the lives of all that are within our reach…it all depends on what seeds we choose to plant and what we want to grow.

WHO CAN I SERVE?

1. Think of a time when you had the opportunity to serve someone, no matter how small it was. Who did you serve, what did you do and how did it make you feel?

2. Name three people that you could serve if you chose to, and what could you do to serve them? (even just to pop in for a chat)

a.
b.
c.

3. Who could you call on the phone that would be absolutely delighted to hear from you?

a.
b.
c.

Even if we spend only five minutes serving others, we can experience the pure long-lasting joy. Sometimes all it takes is a smile to make a difference in someone's day.

I often coach people for free and dedicate my free time to supporting others but I always find so much joy in serving them. When I witness the profound impact I can make on someone's life, just from doing what I love, the rewards far outweigh the time I put in. It brings me pure joy and contentment for which I am truly grateful. To me that is what makes me successful regardless of how much money I earn.

Whatever we seek in life we should give to others first and then we will receive it in return. Perhaps we won't receive it right away, but when we need it most, it will appear.

My friend and neighbour Licia appeared just when I needed her and she gave me all that I needed at the time. If we spend our lives thinking only of ourselves, we can become lost and lonely but if we seek to help others to find what they are looking for, we will get what we want also.

Even in the Bible it says: "Let no man seek his own, but every man another's wealth," and what I believe this means in modern times is if we support and help others to make money, for example, we ourselves will make money; if we lift others up, we will be lifted; if we love with a pure heart, we will be loved purely; if we support others in life, others will support and love us.

Again, we have to treat others as we wish to be treated and we will have all that we need to live a happy and fulfilling life.

Love Lesson #4
My Emotions

"I am a happy and powerful being in control of my happiness, my emotions and my destiny."

One of my greatest attributes is my ability to love all people, but it was also my biggest weakness in life, until I realised that I was the master of my emotions. Only 'I' hold the key to the door of my emotions and only I could allow any amount of love or hate into my heart. Once I realised that I was in complete control of my emotions, my life became better and I was no longer a slave to my circumstances.

Nobody can *make* any of us happy and nobody can make us angry or upset us. When we feel these emotions, it is because we are allowing ourselves to react to our circumstances and are choosing to feel how we feel.

When I first learned this, I thought: *That is nonsense. What a load of rubbish. I can't help feeling the way I do!* But in time I realised it was true, and it gave me a sense of power and control back of my life. Now I know when I feel these negative emotions (which I still do sometimes…I'm not perfect), I am able to come out of it quite quickly because I remind myself of my power.

Sometimes though, we just want to be sad and have a good cry over someone we have lost. We also like to replay all the pain over and over again in our minds even if we know it will hurt us, we are only human, but we have to realise that this is a choice. *We* decide how we react and *we* have chosen to be in our present state of heart and mind. We cannot control our circumstances or always control what happens in our lives, but we can control how we see them and how we react to them.

Gratitude

Gratitude is the very essence of happiness. It's about focusing on what we do have instead of what we don't. When we introduce true gratitude into our lives and hearts, happiness will flow in abundance.

If I had to define the road to happiness in one word it would be gratitude. Daily gratitude practise changed my life. It took me from a place of despair and pain to an abundance of happiness.

We all know about gratitude and what it means. It means giving thanks and appreciating what we already have, but do we really understand the 'power' of gratitude and its effect on our lives? I know I didn't. It was only when I began writing about it, and wholly filling my spirit with what I was truly grateful for, that I began to realise its abounding power in creating a life of abundant joy.

I had been working on my self-awareness and growth when the word gratitude kept popping up and it was calling me to look deeper. Sometimes we think we know what something is but it is only when we delve deeply into it through opening our souls to understanding, that we receive a greater appreciation of its truth.

I had seen a gratitude challenge on social media called #100daysofgratitude and because I love personal challenges. I made a commitment to myself by joining in. From then on, the vision of my life changed as I became aware of my power over my emotions and over my life. For one hundred consecutive days I had committed to post a picture and say what I was grateful for.

It started off easily enough as I talked about the basics of life but as the days went by, I had to look even deeper as not to bore my friends or followers. Doing this publicly on social media was a challenge in itself for me because I am naturally shy, an introvert, so I had to step outside my comfort zone and reveal a part of myself but my intention was to inspire others to find gratitude in their lives also. I had to look beyond the usual things to be grateful for like my home, my family, my health etc. and I would go through each day searching intentionally for things to be grateful for.

My eyes had been looking for things to be grateful for to express my gratitude in the public eye, but as I did so, my heart began to open, to expand in the process, and I could now see the beautiful world that we live in because I was looking with real intent. By nature, I am an honest and genuine person and I cannot lie or make something up just because it would make my life easier, or to make me look better, I had to be genuinely grateful for what I posted about or else it would have not made me feel at peace with myself. And living with a peaceful heart is essential for me in my life.

The best way to describe the feeling that was within me was that I had been given a pair of glasses that allowed me to see things that I couldn't see before. There was more colour, more clarity and more beauty than I had ever seen before and my life was transformed.

Just like we don't know what we don't know, I couldn't see what I couldn't see, but with my new metaphorical 'Gratitude Spectacles' on, and through consciously practising gratitude, I was able to see what I had previously been missing.

Years earlier I had slipped into depression because I had been focusing on what I didn't have, who I had lost, and what I lacked in myself. I wasn't focused on all that I *did* have and all the good within me, I was focused on the empty part of me, the empty part of my broken heart instead of the people and love that were already surrounding me.

I had closed myself in with all the anger and pain within my heart. I felt helpless and alone as I was trapped in a deep dark pit of negativity, but I was too focused on being stuck that I had failed to look up to the light. I was so sad that I had been telling myself untruths such as: "I will never feel love or peace again, nobody cares about me, if I wasn't here nobody would even notice, my heart will never heal, I'm invisible," and so on, but I had been telling myself the wrong stories, and I believed them.

I thought there was no escape because I hadn't been looking for solutions or focused on finding peace, I had been focused on being sad.

I had a family and children that needed me and one day when things couldn't get any worse, I just said, "NADIA... ENOUGH!"

Something that one of my kids said just hit a nerve within me and I realised that I couldn't live like this anymore. It was time to start living again. My children were being affected by my behaviour and my negativity, and I was to blame. I was responsible for their happiness and well-being but what kind of role model was I?

They needed a good example to follow, not the person I had allowed myself to become. My love for them was my fuel and my reason to start looking for the light, to see the blessings that were in my life instead of the pains. I see the depression that I suffered as a blessing also, and I am grateful for every single minute of it because it made me into who I am today. Without it, I would not be able to help others to see the light or be able to write books. Because of it, I learned valuable lessons that gave me the experience and understanding of how to manage my emotions and help others to do the same. No amount of education could have given me what I needed to learn to do what I do. I had to feel it and experience it for myself.

The difference between happy people and unhappy people is not their circumstances, it is their attitude towards their circumstances. For example, imagine two boys that each had a dream of becoming a professional football player and each of them were kicked off their school teams for not being good enough. One could use this as the fuel to work harder, train harder and practise more to prove the coach wrong, determined to never give up, and the other could use it as a sign to quit, to give up on his dream, tell himself that he just isn't good enough and lay down in defeat. Which one of these boys have a better chance of fulfilling their dream?

It's how we choose to look at any given situation that makes the difference. We can focus on how to improve our lives, or focus on how unfair life is. We can focus on what we have, or what we don't, the choice is ours.

We all go through tough times and get stuck from time to time but what can we do?

Gratitude is always a good place to start and we can begin by taking small steps. They say the only way to eat an elephant is one bite at a time and that is how we have to face all our challenges in life.

I took one step at a time to get out of the dark pit that I had put myself in, but every step brought me closer to the light which gave me strength and energy.

The great Chinese philosopher Lao Tzu said, "The journey of a thousand miles begins with a single step," so whether we are taking steps to find ourselves again, to mend our broken hearts, to better our health or working towards living our dream lives, we just have to start...to take a single step.

When we feel our heart is truly broken, we have to find things to be grateful for. For example, if we lose a loved one or have gone through a breakup, we can turn our hearts to gratitude to see things from a positive perspective.

- To realise that we were fortunate to have had these people in our lives for the time that we had them.
- To know that we have learned something valuable from them.
- To be grateful that they loved us and that we loved them.
- To know that neither death nor distance can destroy the love that we once shared.
- To know that we are better and stronger because they were a part of our lives.
- To know that our souls have grown from our experience

In the dark times, we may ask ourselves 'Why me? Why do I have to suffer this pain?' but if we take an honest look around us, we will see that everyone has their own battles in life. We are not unique in that way. We all suffer at times but practising gratitude is a wonderful way to see life with more clarity, and it gives us the fuel to keep us moving forward one step at a time.

We can find gratitude in all life's circumstances if we look for it. We've all heard the example of seeing the glass half full instead of half empty but it isn't always easy. What we focus on becomes what we think about and what we think about becomes who we are. Lao Tzu also said:

> Watch your thoughts they become words.
> Watch your words they become actions.
> Watch your actions they become habits.
> Watch your habits they become character
> Watch your character it becomes your destiny.

We all face difficult times and we all need time to heal but we also need, at some point, to keep moving and keep growing or else we too will lose our lives. From every circumstance we face, we can learn something new about life and about ourselves and there is always an opportunity to grow.

In order to find the good in any situation, we first need to look for it, to seek it out, to see the glass as half full and not focus on the empty part.

The Bible says 'Seek and ye shall find' which means that we will find what we are looking for. So ultimately it all comes down to *what* we are looking for. Are we looking for treasures or poverty? Are we looking for abundance or lack? Are we looking for love or hate? Are we looking for the good or the bad? Whatever we are looking for and focused on, we will find.

Whether we are looking for the good or bad in people or in life for example, we will find it. If we are looking for goodness and love, then we shall find it. If we are looking for reasons that life is so terrible, we will find them also. So being aware of what we are looking for is the deciding factor of what we find and receive in life. Let's do this little experiment:

Wherever you are right now, for ten seconds take a good look around you and look for everything that is brown.

No, don't read on yet. Do the experiment!

Now, once you've got a clear picture of all the brown around you, close your eyes and say out loud everything that you saw that was green and blue!

Hard isn't it?

If you are in a familiar room then you may have been able to name a few items from memory but now look around carefully and you will see all the green and blue that you failed to see. In a picture, in a book cover, in the pattern in a cushion perhaps. The more closely you look, the more you will find. Why didn't you see it before? Because you weren't looking for green and blue, you were looking for brown.

This experiment proves to us that we usually only see what we are actually consciously looking for.

If we go through life focusing on what we do have in our lives – our health, our working legs, the roof over our heads etc. we will realise how fortunate we are already. Alternatively, if we are constantly focusing on what we don't have, we will see only that, and never feel content or feel we have enough in life.

By searching for all that we are grateful for on a daily basis we will be focusing on what we *do* have and all the good things that are already there. Through doing this daily practice, happiness will naturally flow into your life and you will see all the beautiful things and people that are around you because you are consciously looking for them.

I have a gratitude journal (notebook) that I write in first thing every morning to start my day off well. It is a reminder to myself of how grateful I am for all that I have and all that I am.

At the beginning and/or end of every single day it is worth taking the time to write down, with a pen and paper if possible, three things that you are grateful for. It will take only a few minutes out of your day but it will create a lifetime of happiness.

For example:

Today I am grateful for

a. My healthy body and all of its functions to provide me with energy and mobility.
b. My family that loves me unconditionally.
c. My ability to read and write so I can learn and grow in life.

We can all find gratitude in all areas of our lives no matter how unprivileged we may think we are, it all depends what we are looking for.

Completing this next section will help us to see how fortunate we all are in even the basics of life.

1. What are you grateful for and why?

a.
b.
c.

2. Name three people you are grateful to have in your life and why, e.g. my sister that I can turn to in any situation.

a.
b.
c.

3. Name three things you are grateful for to help you to live an easier life, e.g. my car that gives me the freedom to go where I choose, my own room to provide me with personal space.

a.
b.
c.

4. Name three things about your body that you are grateful for, e.g. my eyes that allow me to see, functional legs that allow me to walk.

a.
b.
c.

5. Name three things that you are grateful for in nature, e.g. the hot weather that allows me to swim in the sea, the rain that supplies us with water to drink.

a.
b.
c.

When we focus on what is wrong with our lives and the world, we will see all the bad things which will bring us down. When we focus on what is good, and what is right, then we will feel lighter, brighter and have a heart filled with love and gratitude. Confucius summed up gratitude in this powerful sentence: "I was complaining that I had no shoes until I saw a man with no feet."

Parents

When we are small, we adore our parents and we want to be with them and around them all the time, but as we creep towards our teenage years, we realise that the rules they set are just not fair and we start to wonder if they even like us.

It's no longer just fun and games, our parents force us to do things we don't want to do and we actually have to start doing jobs around the house and start pulling our weight by doing dishes, ironing, cleaning up after ourselves and even others!!! HOW DARE THEY!!!

When my kids were at this stage, I used to joke with them when they started to complain and I would say 'I only had you so I would have someone to help me with the housework. Why else would I have children?' They knew I was joking but I could see them trying to work out if it was actually true or not…LOL.

When I was that age, I used to feel like Cinderella who was slaving away cleaning and ironing while my friends were out playing. I felt like I was a victim and that my mum was a cruel and unkind tyrant. I used to stare out of the window watching my friends play and wonder why I wasn't allowed to go until I'd done my chores. It felt like it just wasn't fair.

Only as a mother did I realise what a gift my mum gave me by making me work. When we have a child, we are given a blessing of a life to bring up in this world. It is our responsibility not only to love them and feed them, but also to teach them and prepare them for a life ahead. A life where we have to work to live. Life doesn't hand happiness, success, riches and good health to only special or lucky people, each and every one of us have to create each of these things. My mum was insistent that my sisters and I work so that we were prepared for life. I learned at a young age that work is a part of life, so it was no longer a chore. The jobs I hated doing, I made into a competition or challenge for myself, and I learned to enjoy working. For example, one of my chores was ironing and I used to have to iron my dad's work shirts that were fiddly, so I used to time myself and set myself goals of how quickly I could do one. I made it fun and it motivated me to work faster so I could go out to play. Even now I look for ways to enjoy the mundane jobs that I still have to do like hanging out the laundry. I put on my headphones and sing and dance my way through all the clothes…I have fun!

So even though I felt like the victim, I am now truly grateful for the lessons that my mum taught me. I opened my own business at 21 years old which I doubt I would have done if I didn't have a good work ethic. I have no fear of chasing my dreams and I have always enjoyed the work that I have done, especially being a full-time mum. I now do as my mum did and give my children chores and responsibilities so that work will come easily to them and they will enjoy their lives doing what they love.

When I was small, I used to be jealous of all the kids that were spoiled. The ones that got everything they wanted whether it was a new bike, lovely trendy clothes, the best toys (nowadays it would be the latest high-tech device), or to go and do whatever they liked. It seemed so unfair. Why do *they* get everything they want and I don't? I also didn't understand the word 'spoiled'. I wondered why the kids that got everything were called 'spoiled' because spoiled meant ruined; damaged; not good any more, but these kids were 'lucky'. It just didn't make sense.

As I grew up and entered adulthood, I began to recognise the pattern in the spoiled kids. They were the ones that struggled the most and couldn't cope with the real world and real life. They discovered that life just doesn't give us what we ask for. They got a real shock when they realised that we all actually have to work for what we want. Our parents are not always around to help us when life gets too hard or to pick us up when we fall and make it all better.

Now as a mother I realise the term spoiled kids… Those poor kids were actually spoiled…duh…and were not given what they actually needed to become independent competent adults. They were ruined and damaged just as the word spoiled meant. Instead of being jealous of these spoiled kids, I should have felt sorry for them. They just couldn't cope and were not sufficiently equipped to go through life, so they struggled and were often led down destructive paths.

My parents had given me the lessons that I needed (even if I didn't understand them at the time), and the survival training that was essential to living in the real world. It would be a bit like being thrown into the jungle with no equipment and no idea what was safe to eat and drink, or how to keep ourselves alive. My kids and I love watching Bear Grylls on the discovery channel and how he teaches his viewers how to survive in various environments, and that is what our parent's job is. Perhaps not to teach us that we can eat worms and get hydrated by squeezing the moisture out of elephant poo, but by *not* giving us whatever we want.

If we were spoiled by our parents and we did get everything we wanted and are now struggling with life, it does not mean that we cannot turn our lives around. And it certainly does not mean that our parents didn't love us or thought they were doing us any harm at the time. From a parental point of view, we all want what is best for our children. We may give in to them to make them happy or to keep the peace, but we would never knowingly or purposely cause any distress to them.

We now live in a material world when we value ourselves by what we have, or own, instead of the quality of our relationships and our levels of personal fulfilment, but true success is found in living life being free to be ourselves and doing what we love. Good communication and connection with those we love is of tremendous value and of far more worth than the latest gadget, but do we even value them?

I remember being about 12 or 13 years old when I had a battle with my parents. There was a school trip to Italy, and of course I wanted to go. My mum and dad refused to let me go so I kicked up an enormous fuss. They said we couldn't afford it but I didn't believe them, we owned our own restaurant and my parents were always working so we had to have money. I thought it was just an excuse so I kept on and on until I got my own way. I eventually managed to guilt them into it and I was over the moon.

It was a fabulous trip and it gave me lots of wonderful memories but now when I think of that trip, it brings tears to my eyes as I remember my dad and the sacrifices he had made for me.

About ten years after that trip, my dad took early retirement, not because we had lots of money but because he had high blood pressure and his health was his priority. Anyway, because he now had a lot of free time on his hands, he decided to write his life story which I had the pleasure of reading at the time. His writings somehow got lost over the years but some of his thoughts and words were imprinted on my heart and will stay with me forever.

In his memoirs, he talked about his childhood and the invasion of Hong Kong by the Japanese. Japan occupied the territory and fishing was forbidden. In his determination to not let his family starve, my grandfather hid under a bridge one day trying to catch a fish but the Japanese soldiers caught him and he was so badly beaten that he never recovered. My dad recounted the story of how he held his father in his arms as he died. At only 17 years old it had become my dad's responsibility to take care of his mother and six younger siblings.

I cried so many tears as I read his words of how he had to leave Hong Kong, his

71

homeland and all he loved to find work to send back money to support his family.

My dad was a quiet man and did not share much about himself or his past but here it was in black and white, the real Frank Wong, my amazing and loving father.

As I read on, I found out that at one time my parents were so broke that they almost lost everything. Of course, it was the time that I wanted to go to Italy. It turned out they really had NO money and were almost bankrupt, yet I would not let it go. My dad wrote about how he didn't have the money to let me go but his heart was breaking to see me so upset. He felt like a failure and a bad father for not being able to give me what I truly wanted. As I read his words, I cried my eyes out and went running to him to ask him why he didn't tell me the truth at the time.

"I would have understood, Dad, if you had explained the situation," I said.

To which he replied, "You were young and you wouldn't have understood."

I persisted, "You should have shown me the bank statements and made it clear. I know I would have been fine with it if I'd known the truth."

"Nadia darling, it was my responsibility. It wasn't your problem, it was mine!"

In the end he had borrowed money from his family, to send me on the trip, and I was none the wiser. I got my way, oblivious to the pain surrounding my family. If I had never read his story, I would never have known the sacrifice he made for me or the torment I put my parents through. I vowed then and there that when I would have children, I was going to talk to them openly and honestly, and to be vulnerable in front of them. Tell them how it is and not try to protect them from the truth, for their sakes as well as my own. I wished I had known the truth and been able to save my mum and dad from a lot of unnecessary heartaches but it was in the past and I had to forgive myself.

Again, I learned from the pain. Knowing how I had treated my parents, gave me the fuel I needed to push forward in my career and business so I could repay them somehow for all the sacrifices they had made for me.

There is no doubt in my mind that I was truly loved even after I put my parents through hell, and be rest assured that you are truly loved too.

My father's words and actions taught me some important life lessons.

1) That we can love our family but not really know what is in their hearts, so we have to look harder.
2) That honest heartfelt communication is essential.
3) To accept that we cannot always have what we want, and to understand that it is for the best, even if we don't agree with it or understand why.
4) That we should all keep some kind of written heartfelt words to leave those we love when we go no matter how old we are.

Writing not only helps us to release the pain and heartache within us which enables us to heal, it is a gift to our future selves and our future generations to learn who we are at different ages and stages in our lives.

If I could have my mum or dad's words here with me now, I would feel them near me and feel their love. After reading my dad's words I knew that one day I would write and share my stories with my children as a gift to them.

My dad's writings were the seeds that led me to having a desire to write many years ago but it took me years to realise that my words were of any worth to the world.

As a mother now, and as I live without my parents' presence, I think of the gift they gave me of life. Their example gives me the inspiration to be an open and loving human being which inspires me to write.

My first book was written as a tribute to them and their amazing influence in my life and in the lives of others. It is a guide and path to live a full and happier life, and an opportunity to leave this world a piece of us, the legacy of what is contained in our hearts through our words, to make the best of life.

There is great beauty within all of us but we have to open our hearts to share it. Let's not just go through life working to make a living, let's work to make a difference.

This is the real meaning of life.

A Mother's Perspective

Something I remind my kids of often is that this is all new to me. Every day and every step I take through life as a mother is a new one. I have never been the mother of a 12-year-old and 15-year-old at the same time before so both my kids and I are walking on an unfamiliar road and doing our best to find the way. I continue to learn, I read parenting books, I ask for advice from experienced mothers so I can be the best mother I can be but being a mother is not the easiest job; however, it is the most rewarding one. Being a mother is the biggest responsibility that the majority of us will ever have, more than being a CEO (chief executive officer) of a large company or owning a hugely successful business. Perhaps being the Prime Minister may be a greater responsibility but you get the point. I ran my own successful business for eight years before I became a mother, which was like a walk in the park in comparison to motherhood, but motherhood gave me greater rewards.

Mothers not only have to take care of your health, teach you how to walk and talk and keep you safe and protect you, we have to teach you how to live in this world, to be the best that you can be and be the happiest you can be, as well as keep a home and feed you. No matter how much we love being a mother, it is exhausting work. So, guess what? We too, make mistakes, get tired and lose our temper. We are not perfect, none of us are, and we don't have all the answers, but we have to listen to our hearts and intuition when it comes to our parenting. WE ARE NOT THE ENEMY and we do not set rules and boundaries to destroy your happiness, but to protect you and teach you the lessons that you need, to be able to deal with the difficulties in life. It's part of your Survival Training.

You may not comprehend our reasoning, and we may even be wrong in certain situations, but we have to live according to our true selves and do what we believe is the right thing to do. Sometimes we have to step back and allow our children to make their own mistakes, to learn the hard way, but it is not easy to sit back and do nothing. No parent wants to see their children suffer, but it may be the only way for them to learn.

Other than having children to fulfil our duty as human beings and to procreate, some of us perhaps have children to be loved and to have someone to shower our love on, but our responsibility goes far beyond that.

Once or twice I have heard the words 'I HATE YOU' aimed at me but my response was something like: "I'm sorry that you hate me but it's my job to protect you and teach you, and I am doing the very best I can with the knowledge that I have.

I may make mistakes but I have to do what I believe is the right thing to do. I'm not here to be loved by you, but to love you whether you love me or not."

I could be a mother that says 'yes' to everything and to always feel loved by them, but I believe that ultimately, they would suffer more. They would not learn how to deal with disappointment or anger and would not be able to deal with life when things don't go their way. We as mothers have to make sacrifices and be the bad one at times for the greater good of our children.

Again, each of us are responsible for our own happiness, and we cannot make anyone happy…but we can make them smile.

The biggest gift you can ever give your parents (whether they are on the earth or have passed), is not success or achievement but living a happy and fulfilling life. To them, you are the brightest star in their universe and all they want is to see you shine!

Shine bright; the world needs your light!

"Life doesn't get better by chance; it gets better by change." – Jim Rohn

If our life and relationships are not where we want them to be, then the only way for them to get better is for *us* to get better. Just as we can't make people feel happy, sad or angry, we can't make them change.

The only thing we can change is ourselves, and then life will get better. We can't keep acting the same way over and over again and expect things to miraculously get better. If something isn't working, then we have to make changes. For example, if we eat junk food on a daily basis and steadily put on the kilos, we can't just hope that one day the excess weight will just disappear, that would be insane. If we want different results in any area of our lives, *we* need to change how we think and what we are doing.

When there is any conflict between you and your parents which is causing you heartache, you have the power to make it better. How? Well, certainly not by complaining or blaming but by taking full responsibility for yourself and the part that you play in the relationship, by being the change. By looking at the situation from their perspective and understanding what their intentions are, you will be able to see every situation with more clarity.

Once we understand that we are on the same team and all want the same result: *Your happiness and well-being*, we can find solutions and welcome compromise to gain harmony and resolve conflict.

1. In your opinion, why do you think your parents set rules and boundaries for you while you were growing up?

2. What do you think your parents' intentions/desires are concerning you and your future? In other words, what do you think they want you to gain from life and why?

3. If you were a parent, what would your intentions be for your children, what would you want for them?

4. If your future children speak to you the way you speak to your parents, how do you think you will feel?

5. What scares you most about being open and honest with your parents?

6. If you were a parent, what kind of relationship would you like to have with your children? How would you like your children to treat you? Why do you want to be treated this way?

7. If you knew that today was the last time you would ever see your parents, what would you want to say to each of them?

8. What can you say or do today to let your parents know how you feel about them and to bring more love into your relationship with each of them?

9. Imagine that your relationship is exactly how you would like it to be and that there is peace and harmony between you and each of your parents. What does it look like, how are each of you acting and behaving? How does it feel to you?

10. What other areas in your life will improve if there is more harmony in your family unit?

Forgiveness

"Love your enemies, bless them that curse you, do good to them that hate you…"
– Matthew 5:44

According to the Collins English dictionary, the word forgive means:

To cease to feel anger and resentment towards a person who has offended, or at an offending deed. To pardon a mistake. To free from a debt.

I believe that forgiveness is less to do with letting the offender off, and more about loving ourselves enough to let go of the pain. Holding on to resentment hurts us, and us alone. There is a famous quote that says, "Holding onto anger is like drinking poison and expecting the other person to die," and that is so true. If we don't let the anger go, it will destroy or kill our sense of peace and love within our hearts and destroy our faith in all people, so we have to learn to let it go.

Lack of forgiveness and holding onto the pain of past events, is like carrying heavy stones in our pockets at all times. Imagine all the injustices of your past are like stones. The bigger and more painful the injustice was, the bigger the stone is.

If we go through life collecting these stones, by holding on to every painful experience, we will be metaphorically filling our pockets. The more we gather, the more we will become weighed down and as we carry this extra load through life, it will eventually stop us from moving forward. It will disable our hearts and minds so we will no longer be able to move freely, and our choices become limited.

The only way to be free and to live the life of our dreams is to empty our pockets and lay the stones to rest.

The same goes when we too need to be forgiven. We make mistakes also and may not deliberately mean to hurt others so we have to empty our pockets to free ourselves from the heavy stones that we are carrying, to give us the peace and freedom we all deserve.

We cannot force others to repent of their wrongdoings but we can stand up and take responsibility for ours, and apologise.

Some people can hang on to the past and their pain for decades, but if they continue to allow themselves to be the victim, they will stay the victim. They cannot change the past but they can change how they look at life, and change the future. We all get to choose whether to allow our past to destroy us or to strengthen us. If we are in pain because of guilt for our own wrongdoings we have to forgive ourselves and let it go, and if we can make things right, we should.

One of my childhood classmates/friends had a hard time at primary school because he was picked on, and singled out, by a teacher. From the age of five he was given the belt regularly (hit really hard with a thick leather strap on the hand) for being bad. In those days it was known as discipline, these days it would be called abuse.

Because of this, he became aggressive, behaved really badly and used to bully other kids as he didn't know how to deal with his emotions. At one time he even kicked me in the face and split my lip but I didn't hold it against him. He wasn't a nice child but we all accepted him. There were only ten of us in our class, so we were like a little family. He did, however, treat my sister badly and she hated him for hurting me…and lots of people hated him, kids and teachers alike, so he was used to feeling disliked.

Anyway, we all grew up and went our separate ways but many years later, we found ourselves with the same group of friends and we reconnected. He talked about how horribly he had treated people in his youth and how he was trying to make things right which I really admired. He had contacted a few of his 'victims' and apologised for his behaviour which not only allowed him to free himself of his guilt, but brought peace to all concerned. He even attended the wedding of one of his victims as they had become good friends. He stood up and faced his mistakes and took responsibility for his past even though he was only a child.

When I told my sister this, she just said she didn't believe he had changed so dramatically because he had made her life hell, but I suggested that we all meet for a drink and she reluctantly agreed. As soon as he saw her, he walked straight up to her with open arms and said

"I'm sorry, Gisella, I treated you really badly and you did not deserve to be treated that way. Can you please forgive me?"

What could she say? She was struck dumb by his honesty and remorse, and the fact that he made no excuses for his behaviour. He had been wrong and admitted it and she respected him for taking responsibility for his actions. Both my friend and my sister emptied some stones out of their pockets that day and it was wonderful to be a witness to it.

The Art of Forgiveness

Some of us find forgiving others a simple task, and some of us may need to work a little harder at it, but we can all learn to forgive just as we can learn any new skill or art. When we ask ourselves the right questions, we can begin to see that none of us are perfect and we are all in need of forgiveness.

I remember watching a documentary a few years ago about a man that was in a horrific car accident with his family and sadly he lost his wife and two of his children. I can't even imagine how he felt after he found out that the accident was caused by a 17-year-old drunk driver. The young man had foolishly jumped into his parents' car without a licence while intoxicated and drove straight into this poor family's car destroying their lives in an instant.

The tears were streaming down my cheeks as I watched this father going to visit the young man about a year after the incident in a correctional facility for young offenders. He embraced the young man and told him that he had forgiven him. The young man was sobbing and full of remorse as he knew he didn't deserve to be forgiven for his incredibly thoughtless behaviour. The two men embraced and cried together. Each of them needed forgiveness in order for them to move forward in life and to continue living. Their lives would never ever be the same but they had to let go of the pain.

The father still had one remaining child which gave him the strength to carry on and keep living but he had been so angry. The bitterness and anger had eaten away at his soul until the pain became unbearable. It was then that he realised that he had to face this young man in order to let go of the terrible resentment that he was carrying, for his own sake and for the sake of his child. Seeing this young man and feeling his sense of remorse and pain allowed the father to let go. He realised that this was no evil being, just a child that needed to be forgiven.

As hard as it was, forgiveness and love were the only way forward.

Watching this and hearing each of the men speak about how they felt really pulled at my heartstrings as I couldn't even imagine how hard it was for either of them to feel peace. None of us can go back and change the past, so we have to move forward with love in our hearts in the best way that we can.

I like to go through life looking for the good in people instead of the bad. After all, we usually find what we are looking for. If people are unkind or treat me badly, I ask myself what they must have gone through to be acting this way towards me. I wonder how deeply unhappy they must be, or question the condition of their mental health. The quality of our lives is determined by the choices that we make. We all make bad choices from time to time but that doesn't necessarily make us bad people.

I'm not talking about the horrific and terrifying acts of evil in the world today but that which are in our day-to-day lives.

Answering the questions below will enable us to be more aware of our thinking and learn how to empty our pockets by laying down some of the heavy stones that have been weighing us down in the past.

It takes conscious effort and work to make improvements in our lives but we will benefit greatly by freeing ourselves of pain. We can then continue to move forward in our lives regardless of whether the people that have wronged us feel any sense of remorse or not.

We are all human and we all make mistakes, so each and every one of us needs to be forgiven at times in life. We all have 'off' periods when we are not at our best but that does not make us bad people or mean that there is hatred within us, it just means we are temporarily out of balance.

The quote that reminds me to be more forgiving is: 'ONLY HURT PEOPLE,

HURT PEOPLE!' When I think of all the times I have hurt others in the past, it was always because I was so hurt myself and I was fighting back. I didn't go out of my way to deliberately hurt anyone.

Again, we have to "Treat others as we wish to be treated", so we have to forgive others if we want to be forgiven.

How Forgiving Am I?

1. On a scale of 1–10, how forgiving are you? (1 being I never forgive people that hurt me, 10 being I do my best to let go and see the good in every situation)

    a.   Towards others?
    b.   Towards yourself?

2. Think of a time when someone upset you, how did you feel? Angry? Disappointed? Let down? Hurt? Describe how you felt.

3. Do you believe that the person that hurt you did it intentionally? In other words, did they deliberately go out of their way to upset you? Why do you believe this?

4. What other reason could they have had for the way they treated you that had nothing to do with you personally? (Perhaps they were suffering themselves, scared, felt alone or were angry at someone else.)

5. Why do you think they did what they did or said what they said? (Was it from malice or from a place of pain, from lack of knowledge and understanding about the situation or because they were unhappy and insecure in themselves) Explain.

6. Think of a time when you upset someone or hurt them. How did you feel about the way you behaved? Did you hurt them deliberately? Why did you hurt them? How did it make you feel? If you could go back, what would you do differently?

7. Who in your past do you need to let go of, or forgive?

8. Who do you need to ask for forgiveness from?

Imagine a boat that is docked at the port that is ready to leave, no amount of manual labour or fuel will move that boat away from the port until it is untied and freed from the dock.

Just as the rope needs to be untied or cut for the boat to be free, we also need to cut the ties of wrongdoings and past relationships in our lives to be free, and we can do this through forgiveness.

'Letting go' gives us the freedom to sail off into the sunset towards a better life.

Letting Go

Once we fully comprehend that we control our emotions, we will realise the power we have over the quality of our lives, but in order to be totally free to be ourselves, we first have to let go of some of the things that are holding us back such as:

1) Limiting beliefs
2) Negativity and complaining
3) Blame
4) Telling ourselves false stories
5) The past
6) Comparison...comparing ourselves to others
7) Perfection
8) Things we can't control

1. Limiting Beliefs

Abraham Lincoln supposedly said, "A man is usually about as happy as he has made his mind up to be." and I believe this to be true. We become who we believe we are in our minds. Whether that is happy, successful and lovable, or a miserable loser and unlovable, we live up to who we believe we are. What we believe determines the quality of our lives.

We hear of miracles all the time of people being told they may never walk again due to illness or injury but against all odds, they manage to walk again because they refused to see the vision the doctors had created, and created their own vision with a better ending. With a lot of faith and belief, consistent hard work and never giving up, they got the results they wanted. The same goes for our happiness, it all depends on what we believe.

One of my dear friends once said to me, "I will never be happy," and it broke my heart to see him this way because I knew that until he decided on a different fate for himself, it would most likely be true. *He* had created this limiting belief that was fixed in his mind, it was not the truth but it was *his* truth. He had used his past experiences, and his lack of understanding and faith, to create an unhappy ending to his story. A story that he was writing.

We put the limits on ourselves by perhaps listening to the opinions of others. We convince ourselves that we can't do certain things and we even come up with some fantastic excuses to confirm our own prognosis, but the only true limits we have are in our minds. For example, because I was a wheezy child and had breathing difficulties, I believed that I couldn't run. And guess what? I could not run. I had tried many times but because I became out of breath too easily, I stopped trying. When I was diagnosed as an asthmatic, it all made sense. As I watched others run in awe of them, I knew that this was not my fate and I accepted that I will never be able to run. I had asthma.

Over the next few years, I changed my whole lifestyle and was fit and well, but I still believed that I couldn't run. It was so fixed in my mind.

Only when I began learning how much power we have over our lives, I realised that I had placed barriers in all areas of my life, including my inability to run. So, at the age of 45, I decided to put it to the test. When I was out walking, I started to run for a few metres at a time. I began slowly and each day I ran a little more. 100 metres, 200 metres, 300 metres and so on until I managed to run a whole kilometre. It did not happen overnight and it was not always easy but I consistently kept working at it. Within a few weeks, I was running 3 km three times a week and I was ecstatic. I set myself a yearly goal from then on to run at least 365km a year, representing 1 km for every day and I have done so ever since. If I had held on to limiting beliefs then, this would never have happened. I love running, it's my meditation time. It's my place of pure freedom and a reminder of my personal power over my life.

Letting go by removing my limiting beliefs allowed me to fulfil a longing within myself. I now believe that anything is possible with belief, consistent hard work and determination.

- What limiting beliefs have you been telling yourself that holds you back? What would you love to do or be but tell yourself that you can't?

2. Negativity

This too is a harmful habit we should let go of. We don't necessarily do it purposefully, and we all get ourselves into a negative mindset from time to time but we need to get out as soon as possible before we drag ourselves down, and others with us. It's easy to complain but it gets us absolutely nowhere. When I think of negativity it reminds me of Winnie the Pooh and friends. When my son was small, he had a Tigger toy phone and when we pressed the buttons, all the characters used to speak. Tigger would call up and say "It's a lovely day for a picnic, would you like to come?" all the replies were happy and positive except for Eeyore the donkey. He replied "It'll probably rain at the picnic" in a slow and miserable tone.

We can choose who we want to be in life and we can either choose to be like the fun loving bouncy and cheerful Tigger, or Eeyore who likes to steal everyone's joy. I choose to be Tigger *and* I would also choose to be around Tigger, to be his friend. In Love Lesson#1 we talked about what kind of person you want to *be* and what kind of person you want to *be around,* so if you chose to be with cheerful and energetic people, then others may feel the same.

I started coaching someone new this week and one of her issues is that she has very few friends and feels that they don't include her in things, so I asked her what kind of person she would like to be around and she said… "someone positive and cheerful". As soon as she said the words out loud, she understood that the reason that others don't include her is because she is not *being* the kind of person she would like to spend time with. She realised (without any input from me) that if she wants to see change, she has to *be* the change. We are all happy to listen to others problems but for how long? An hour, a day, a month, a year, several years? If any of you have overly negative friends you will know that no matter how much you love them and want to be there for them, they are energy draining, and we naturally want to limit the time we spend with them because they can suck the life out of us after a while. We have to give ourselves a check-up from time to time to ask ourselves if we are radiating energy or draining it from those surrounding us. Cheerfulness creates energy and invites warm and loving people into our lives and negativity blocks that. Who wouldn't want to be around someone who radiates energy?

We have control over who we want to be and over our emotions, but we have to use our personal power to make changes within ourselves. Just like we won't lose excess weight without changing something within our daily habits, we won't just become positive. *We* have to let go of our negative thoughts, stop focusing on what we don't have or what is bad, and look for the good in everything and everyone.

'Seek and you shall find…' whatever we look for, we will find (remember the colour experiment). Look for all the wonderful things in life like Tigger, or look for all that is wrong, or could go wrong, like Eeyore. Look for the light in life or the darkness, the choice is ours. We just need to decide which one we want to have.

• Who are you most like, Tigger or Eeyore? Which one of them would you choose to be around and why?

3. Blame

When things don't go as we'd hoped we want to understand why, so we start to play the blame game. We pick our way through the situation and say things like

"If he hadn't done that to me, then I wouldn't have reacted the way I did" or "I'm miserable because of them, it's their fault", but the reality is that whatever has happened has happened, and we cannot change the past, only focus on finding a solution or letting it go.

Blaming others is a complete waste of energy and time, and resolves nothing. People make mistakes; we make mistakes and we are all guilty at times. We blame others for our pain, making us angry, for hurting our feelings etc. but we can choose how we feel and how we react to any situation. Problems and misunderstandings most often happen over time through a series of events so not only one party is to blame, we all play our part and none of us are perfect. The old adage "don't cry over spilt milk" means don't get upset over something that has already happened. It was an accident and very rarely would a person deliberately spill milk. When it is done, it is done. We can't un-spill the milk but we can all clean up the mess.

Knowing who made the mistake doesn't change the final outcome so there is no point to blame. Blaming others is like trying to hand them the guilt to carry around like stones in their pockets like wrongdoings, but if we still carry the anger towards them, then we have to carry the weight too.

If we treat others as we wish to be treated, we have to ask ourselves: "Would I want to carry my mistakes and errors like a heavy chain around my neck?" If not, then think about how you would like to be treated in this situation.

• Who or what do you tend to blame when things don't go your way on a daily basis? Why do you think it is their fault and what can you focus on instead of blaming?

4. Telling Ourselves False Stories

I for one can be guilty of this at times, I think we all can, but I remind myself to stop it because it will only hurt *me*. When somebody says something or does some-thing and we don't understand why, we invent false stories/ scenarios in our heads of what we think it could be instead of waiting for the truth. This is a dangerous path to go down because we will make up the biggest horror stories with no real evidence to back them up and create a whole lot of mess. Our brains are naturally curious and we want to get to the truth, but if we don't get answers, we often fill in the blanks ourselves.

I once heard a story of a man that was on his way home, on his daily commute on the train, when a man and his four kids jumped on. Before they came on, the man had been enjoying the peace while reading his book but these four kids were running around and making a lot of noise. The father just sat in silence saying nothing with his head down, practically ignoring the kids. The man was furious and thought to himself: *What kind of father is he? Those children are terrible and they should be told off. They need to be disciplined,* and so on. The father looked up and saw the look of anger and disgust on the man's face and turned to him and whispered:

"I am so sorry if the kids are disturbing you, I have just picked them up and I'm taking them home. I have been at the hospital all day with their mother and now I'm sitting here trying to work out how to tell them that they will never see their mother again, she died this afternoon."

After offering his sincere condolences, the man sat back and felt terrible for what he had previously thought but it taught him a valuable lesson. That we do not know what is going on in the lives of others so we cannot judge. He had made up his mind about this father (made up a story), and had gotten so angry for no reason, all because he wanted some peace.

We also have to quit the 'He Thinks / She Thinks' stories that we tell ourselves. Some examples of this are:

He thinks I'm lazy.
She thinks she is clever but…
They think they are better than me.
I think she doesn't like me.
She wouldn't want to go out with me.
He thinks that I don't like him.
They will think I'm boring if I don't do what they want me to do.

Unless the person concerned has actually told us what they think, *we have no idea what they are actually thinking.* We are not mind readers, so none of us know what others are thinking, we are just telling ourselves false stories. When there is no real evidence at a crime scene and no witnesses, there is no case.

Most of our doubt and conflict doesn't come from what has been said, but come from us telling ourselves false stories. Being more aware of what is truth and what is speculation will help us to see life more clearly.

• What false stories have you ever told yourself? When did you say something like 'they think' without any clear evidence to back it up?

5. The Past

Our past is often the hardest thing to let go of, but by letting go we are essentially removing the lead boots that weigh us down and prevent us from moving forward. We hang on to people (and situations) in our hearts from the past and letting go may take a little work. Even though we know that we will emerge feeling bad, we still allow ourselves to go to that place in our minds to re-live all the beautiful (or most painful moments) of our past. We know we have to move on but sometimes, we just don't want to let go.

Our memories are a library of our emotional history, where we register the best and worst parts of the people that have touched our lives and we store them in our minds. We keep them in our personal library of all past experiences for us to go to remember, if and when they are needed.

When we go to look for something to cheer us up, we go to the happy section of the library and search for the fun times we had and relive them in our minds to make us smile.

When we look for a reason to remind us how awful life is, we go to the horror section and relive all our darkest times to remember the pain we suffered. Somehow, we like to keep going back to this section over and over again which makes no real sense. It would be like watching one of the worst movies you have ever watched, over and over again.

We each have our own personal library that only we have access to, and we are free to choose which of our emotions we want to experience again. But the question is, what department of the library of our minds are we spending most of our time in?

Self-development (growth)
History (the past)
Horror (our darkest moments)
Drama (our trials)
Romance (loving relationships past or present)
Thriller (our adventures)
Study (learning new things)
Comedy (the laughs that we have experienced)

If we spend the majority of our time in the horror section of our libraries, it's only natural that we will feel low and feel stuck in life. Whatever we focus on, we will see. If we are looking back constantly, it's only natural that we can't see what is in front of us. In order for us to get anywhere in life we have to keep facing forward.

Imagine getting into a car and driving ourselves to where we want to go. What do you think would happen if we were looking backwards? It is fine to look back from time to time to remind us of how far we have come or to make sure we are on track, but if we keep our eyes focused on what is behind us, how can we ever get where we want to be? Where would we end up? Either nowhere (and stay stuck) because we never even moved, or crashed into the back of someone risking hurting ourselves and others.

I love Life Coaching because instead of focusing on the problems in life, we focus on the solutions. Instead of looking back at our mistakes, we focus on where we want to go and work out how to get there.

It's like drawing a line in the sand and saying; this is the starting point and then going on an amazing life adventure. There will be ups and downs but we can live each day learning new things, meeting new people and growing more. We are able to enjoy life in the present, not living in our past, reliving the pain over and over again.

We all have a past and the older we get the bigger the past, but no matter who we are or how old we are, the past is always behind us. All the good and bad that we have gone through has taught us what we needed to get us here, exactly where we are meant to be.

The old song *"Che sera sera…whatever will be will be"* means that some things we cannot change so we have to let it be. That we have to accept certain outcomes are just meant to be, but we also cannot sit around hoping that life will magically improve.

We have to take a step forward if we want to move forward.

We have to let go and cut the ties of the past, especially in our broken relationships. We like to torture ourselves when it comes to lost love and we not only hold on to the past, we go out of our way to remind ourselves of what we have lost. We look back at the photos, we listen to the songs that remind us of them and even check their every move on social media, but the honest truth is, if they wanted us in their lives, they would be here. It is that simple. We cannot wait for life to just get better in any of life's situations, *we* have to turn in the right direction and take the steps forward to make life better.

Sometimes I do this little exercise in my mind to help me to lay down some metaphorical stones to lessen my load (when I inadvertently pick up heavy stones).

I find a peaceful quiet spot and sit or lay with my eyes closed. I take some long deep belly breaths in and out through the nose (Belly breath meaning my belly swells when I breathe in, and goes down when I breathe out).

I then imagine myself in a beautiful green park on the river. I am the only one there and I find an enormous tree where I lay my stones to rest. I don't bury them; I just lay them down on the grass and know I can go and visit whenever I choose. This is my peaceful place. It is my sanctuary. I imagine myself removing the heavy stones from my pockets laying down my pain, my past and my love for all those that are no longer in my life. I send love and light to them all and wish them peace and love whether they are living or have passed.

Sometimes I cry if I need to, but I always feel lighter and leave with love and light in my heart.

This is me and this is how I am able to let go of the past. I also write down how I am feeling to unburden myself of my heavy load. We can put it to the back of our minds or bury the pain of the past within ourselves and tell ourselves we are over it but it can be easier said than done. In order for us to be free we need to set the pain free. Sometimes we find the stones back in our pockets again but we just have to revisit our peaceful place, lay them down again and walk away with a more peaceful heart.

In my life experience, the times of great pain and sorrow, are followed by a greater understanding of myself and my purpose in life. It was in my pain that I found the better and stronger version of me that I grew to love. When I took responsibility for my own happiness, I was able to let go of the past and move on.

• What areas of your past do you need to lay to rest?

6. Comparison

The only comparison we should make is with ourselves. From who we are now, to who we can become, so that one day we can stand tall and proudly say: " I am a beautiful human being!"

I talk a lot about comparison in this book because we need a constant reminder of how it is detrimental to our growth, especially in the world of today. In the past, people only had the few people around them to compare themselves with but with social media, we are now comparing ourselves to millions of other people that we know nothing about. If we are not comparing our looks, we are comparing our intelligence levels, our qualifications, our popularity etc. but it is holding us back.

Imagine running in a 100m race and instead of focusing on the finish line and doing *your* best, you keep looking at your competitors to see where they are in fear of them beating you. How well do you think you would do compared to someone focusing on their actual performance?

If we want to succeed in life, we have to focus on being *our* best, not keep looking at what others are doing unless of course we hope to learn from them. We all have unique gifts and talents, and we all have our own life's purpose. No two of us are the same but we are all equal in value. Understanding that none of us are better than or less than another will help us to stop comparing ourselves to others. We all have something different to offer the world and we all shine in our own way.

Another way to help us to understand that making comparisons serves no purpose is to think of your favourite foods. For example, my favourite foods are my homemade healthy ice cream and sushi, but how can I possibly compare them? How can I choose which one is best because I love each of them equally? Whichever I choose to eat depends on how I feel and what my body needs at the time. Each of them serves me in a different way and neither of them is better or worse than the other. They are both delicious to my palate so there is no comparison.

We too serve our own purpose in life and are appreciated in the same way. Whether we are sushi or ice cream, some will love us and some won't understand how delicious we are, but it doesn't make us less delicious!

• When you catch yourself comparing yourself to others, what are you going to tell yourself?

7. Perfection

This wasn't an easy one for me to let go of and it took a bit of time to master. I had been a perfectionist my whole life and was actually quite proud of myself and the quality of my standards. I thought I was striving to be the best I could be, but I was striving to be perfect and therefore setting myself up to fail, because PERFECTION DOES NOT EXIST. Whenever I was less than 100% to my standards, I felt I wasn't good enough.

Of course, we would all love to be naturally beautiful, have great bodies, be intelligent, be popular, be loved, be in a wonderful relationship, be successful and have material wealth among other things simultaneously but for me, if I wasn't all of these things, I felt like a failure. I was striving for an unrealistic outcome because perfection does not exist.

We each have our own gifts and talents, our own strengths and weaknesses and our own unique personalities but *none of us are perfect*.

When I moved to Italy, I struggled with the language. Even though my mum was Italian, she never spoke to us in Italian so I never learned. My sister was living here in Italy and she had picked it up right away but for me, it was a whole other story. That was when the self-doubt began to creep in. I began taking Italian classes but I soon discovered that it didn't come naturally to me, and the more classes I went to, the more confused I became. I noticed all the words that I had been using were not grammatically correct so I was scared to say anything at all in case I made more mistakes.

A couple of thoughtless people had made comments about how badly I spoke considering I was half-Italian, so I stopped trying.

I allowed my fear of failure, other people's unkind comments and my own perfectionism to block me. I spent the next ten years getting by, using only a hand full of words but I slowly lost *all* of my self-confidence.

I had let my fear of not being perfect and making mistakes hold me back and I closed myself in. I got used to saying very little and as my kids grew, they began to speak for me.

When I was young, I used to criticise my Chinese granny for years because after living in the UK for 20 plus years, she never spoke English. I thought, *How can she possibly live in a country for all these years and not speak the language?* I had told myself (a false story) that she had either made a choice not to learn and not to fit in, or that she could actually speak but made a choice not to speak to us, her grandchildren.

The mind really does like to make up stories to support our judgements, doesn't it? I hadn't once considered that she was afraid or lacking in self-confidence. I hadn't considered that she may have had real learning difficulties or real struggles that prevented her from trying. Only when I was struggling myself did I think about how hard it must have been for her and I learned another valuable lesson about not judging others.

When I started to gain my personal power back years later, I learned to give up on perfection and just do it anyway. To be courageous doesn't mean that we have no fear, it means we have to face our fears and do it anyway.

What was the worst that could happen? People can criticise me again, they can laugh at me, they can judge me but they cannot stop me. I started speaking anyway, and finally started to build relationships and my life got better and better. I made a ton of mistakes and I still do, but the difference is that now I don't care. I laugh at myself and keep on talking.

Perfection is not real in any area of life, in our looks, our bodies, our relationships, our talents etc. and we have to let it go to be truly free. Perfection only exists in the minds of each individual and what seems perfect to us could be a disaster to another. So instead of striving to be perfect, we need to strive to be the best that we can be, focus on our strengths, not on our weaknesses and be better today than we were yesterday.

- What ideas of perfection do you need to let go of that are preventing your personal freedom?

8. Things we can't control

We have so much more control over our lives than we think we have but there are certain things in life that are entirely out of our hands, and are in the hands of God. Spending time worrying over things that we cannot change or wishing they were different, is a waste of our precious time and energy, and causes our bodies unneeded stress, which can lead to illness.

- We cannot control what bodies we are born into, but we can appreciate and respect the bodies that we do have.
- We cannot control the planet's natural disasters but we can take responsibility for how we treat the environment through our own use of plastic etc.
- We cannot control the hatred and war in the world, but we can each be an example of goodness and kindness within our families and communities.
- We cannot change the behaviour of others but we can be an inspiration by the way we behave towards them.
- We cannot control how other people feel about us but we can still love with an open heart without expecting anything in return.
- We cannot control whether or not we will get a serious incurable illness, but we can take care of our health in the best possible way by consuming only clean and healthful foods and drinks, to give us the best chance of recovery or quality of life.
- We cannot control whether we are born with full functioning body parts but we can be an inspiration to others by still living a full and happy life.

One of the most inspiring people I have ever come across is Nick Vujicic. One of his videos popped into my social media feed when I needed it the most (no coincidence), and I instantly fell in love with his soul and energy (Google him…he is amazing).

Nick was born with no arms and no legs but with two small feet one of which had two toes. He suffered terribly as a child and even attempted to take his own life by drowning but when he realised that he was not the only person in the world with his disability, he realised he could be an inspiration to others. In spite of the cards that he was dealt, he created an amazing life that many of us feel we could only dream of. He is married with four children, an international motivational speaker, a bestselling author and travels the world inspiring others. He is a true example of love and grace, and lives a full and happy life. He manages to write with his toes, types on his keyboard, and also swims, all things that we take for granted. He used to pray for arms and legs as a child but eventually accepted that God had different plans for him.

Nick is a truly inspirational man that had suffered more than most of us will ever know but did not use his disability as an excuse not to live, he faced life with courage and won. He embraced his trials, overcame doubt and fear, and shines brightly in the world to show others the way.

I can't speak for him but I can imagine that as he serves others, he is lifted with pure joy knowing what a difference he is making to the world. A true hero in my eyes!

Letting go of what we cannot control and looking at life from a different perspective gives us the strength to overcome trials in life. Instead of wasting our time saying it's not fair, 'Why me?' we have to seek out what we can give to others, how we can lift others and how we can make a difference.

We are all here for a reason and we all have to grow through what we go through to give us experience to make us better. We have to trust that God has his reasons, even if we don't yet understand them.

Because we are all blessed with free will, we can either choose to swim in our own misery soup or to climb out, shake ourselves off and spread our wings to fly to greater heights. We cannot always change our circumstances but we all have the ability to fly.

• What area do you need to work on 'letting go' of that is holding you back the most? What can you start doing to start making a difference today?

How to Deal with Anger

Anger is a powerful emotion that can destroy everything in its path if we let it. When we go through certain stages of growth in life, our bodies have to adapt to changing hormones and all new emotions come into play. Of course, we don't know how to handle them as we don't even understand what they are until we experience them. One minute we can be fine and the next we can be raging over something trivial.

According to Chinese medicine (my husband is a Chinese medicine practitioner and acupuncturist), emotions are connected to certain organs. For example, joy comes from the heart (which we all know) but anger comes from the liver. So, our moods can change according to the level of heat or imbalance we have in our liver at any given time due to various factors such as our hormone levels, what we eat and drink, our levels of stress, our health etc. Our bodies store toxins in the liver so the cleaner we eat and the less toxins we put into our system, the more balanced our livers can be so we feel not only healthier but happier too. Regardless of how much we weigh and the shape of our bodies, eating processed foods has an undeniable negative effect on us. Understanding this helps me to realise that anger can be a physical reaction and not just an outburst of hatred. It doesn't make an angry outburst acceptable, but it does make it forgivable, especially if the anger is aimed at us. Remembering that we cannot make a person feel any emotion helps us not to take it personally. It is their imbalance, it is their lack of control, or perhaps it is a cry for help or attention. We may not be able to control the physical manifestation of our own anger in our liver but we are in full control of whether we express our anger openly and take it out on someone else, or manage it in other ways. Again, it's about making the right choices.

Let's for a minute imagine anger as being a forest fire. In the right environment, it can spread and destroy miles and miles of land leaving nothing but dust and ashes if no attempts are made to contain it in some way.

Anger can do the same to our lives and relationships if we allow it to spread without making any effort to manage it. It will consume anything or anyone that comes into contact with it and people will stay well away so they do not get burned.

Just as fire needs sufficient fuel to burn, so does anger. If someone is verbally taking their anger out on us, we should stay at a safe distance and avoid throwing fuel on it by speaking or reacting. We are human and it's only natural for us to feel the need to defend ourselves or to attempt to put the fire out but saying anything will just be adding more fuel. The only thing we could say to perhaps put out the fire is something like "You are right, I am wrong" and then say nothing more and stay back and wait it out. When a fire runs out of fuel it will eventually calm down and burn itself out.

Anger to me is a feeling of being powerless over a situation or the actions of others and therefore a cry of frustration, or a cry for help. A feeling of not being able to cope with a situation.

Even though I believe that anger is more about feeling powerless than a hateful act, when I am the recipient, I can sometimes feel victimised, want to defend myself and fight back but experience has taught me to walk away as I remind myself that this isn't about me, it's about them.

When things don't go the way we hope they will, like I mentioned earlier, we tend to look for someone to blame and play the blame game but as a recipient, if we are not willing to play the game by fighting back, their efforts will be futile.

If we are that fire however and we are carrying the anger, the best thing we can do is to isolate it so nobody gets hurt. Just as other people's anger is not about us, our anger is not about them and we need to regain our power over our emotions and understand what we are feeling powerless about. We can then let go of the negative thoughts that are fuelling our feelings. First, we need to put out the fire but how?

We are all so diverse and each of us have to find what works for us but first we need to physically remove ourselves from the space that we are in and create a fresh clean space preferably outdoors if we can and get some fresh air. Here are a few suggestions that work for me:

- Go for a walk-in nature by myself (being near water helps to calm me down)
- Go for a run
- Go for a swim
- Listen to a guided meditation on YouTube
- Plug in my earphones and listen to my favourite dance tunes and dance the anger away
- Go somewhere quiet, listen to some calming music and do some deep belly breathing
- Pray for a peaceful heart

Movement and Mood

Tony Robbins is in my opinion one of the greatest, kindest, loveable men on this entire planet, and he talks about how our emotion is controlled by motion and he is absolutely right. The way we move effects the way we feel. There is no doubt about it.

When we are moving our bodies enough it is hard to feel really upset, angry or depressed because it helps us to release our emotional pains and free our spirits. It seems to be common knowledge that exercise is a mood booster and makes us feel happier but how many people put this information to the test?

Even the way we carry ourselves effects our moods. For example, when we feel down, we sit down, lie down, walk with our shoulders down, our arms hang down, our heads are down even our mouth turns down so it's no wonder we feel so bad. But the moment we look up, sit up, jump up and stand straight up, we start to pick up. If we feel down or lacking in self-confidence all we need to do is to dress as if we are confident, walk tall with our head up and a big smile and boom – we will feel confident. You don't believe me?

Let's do a few little experiments to test this theory.

> Sit slumped in your chair for a minute, round your shoulders, let your chin drop, your hands drop and your jaw hang. On a scale of 1–10 (1 being the lowest and 10 being the highest)

How attractive do you feel?
How energetic do you feel?
How cheerful do you feel?

Now let's do the opposite. Sit up straight, shoulders back chin up and put a great big smile on your face. On a scale of 1–10

How attractive do you feel?
How energetic do you feel?
How cheerful do you feel?

I don't know about you but my levels were significantly higher on the second test. Try this with your friends and family to see the difference in the way they feel.

> For this little experiment you'll need a small mirror, if you don't have one handy put your camera on selfie mode to see your reflection. Now put your chin down and look at your face without smiling and rate on a scale of 1–10

How powerful do you feel?
How attractive do you feel?
How confident do you feel?

Now look at yourself while holding the mirror slightly above eye level with your chin up.

How different do you feel compared to when you were looking down?
In which position did you feel happier and more confident?

> ➢ Now for an acting class. Please don't skip this section as it is very significant to what I'm saying. I'm not trying to make you feel foolish…honest.

Let's imagine for a minute you are depressed, sad and feeling miserable. Now stand up and walk around the room as if you are miserable. What are your eyes focused on, straight ahead or the floor? What position is your head in, up or down? How are you holding your shoulders, back or slumped?
 Write down how this makes you feel? (Use the table below as a guide if need be)

• I feel:

In contrast: You are now a Super Hero. Spend a couple of minutes walking around the room with your fists firmly placed on your hips, your head up and your imaginary cape waving gently behind you as you walk (hard not to smile huh?).
 Again, write down how you feel by moving your body in a more positive position? (Again, using the table as a guide if needed)

• I feel:

cheerful	confident	enthusiastic	powerful
excited	happy	elegant	strong
unstoppable	brave	positive	bright
attractive	weak	unhappy	expendable
powerless	useless	unattractive	joyful
beautiful	pathetic	stagnant	negative
inspired	energised	passionate	sad
loved	important	valued	significant
miserable	overjoyed	insignificant	alive

• What did you learn about yourself when doing these experiments?

Ask and It Shall Be Given. Maybe.

We have talked about and experienced how we can make ourselves feel better through the way we think and the way we move, which demonstrates how much power we actually have over our emotions, ourselves and our lives. But something that we cannot control is the actions of other people, their behaviour and response towards us, so we also have to learn to ask for what we need from them and from life.

At times we can feel upset because we don't get what we want whether it be attention, love, time or help from others, but IF WE DON'T ASK, WE DON'T GET! None of us are mind readers so we cannot possibly know the needs of another human being.

Even mothers don't always know the needs of their babies. When babies cry, it is their way of communicating with their mother to tell them they need something, but what? The mother then goes through all the possible reasons. Are they hungry, thirsty, do they need their nappy changed, do they need comfort and attention? When they work out what is needed, they can then tend to their baby's needs. This goes on constantly for the first few months and it can be exhausting. Once babies begin to be more alert, they start to communicate in their own way that sometimes only their mother can understand, and then gradually start to use words to express their needs. This is human nature and mothers are only too happy to tend to their growing children.

The problem with us as human beings though is that sometimes, we continue to go through life without actually communicating effectively, and just continue to cry (moan and complain) or sulk when we need something and don't get it automatically. Even though we have the skills to communicate and express our feelings, we don't use them, yet we still expect our needs to be met. We somehow think the other person should know what we want but we are being unrealistic. Wouldn't you rather someone asked for what they need from you instead of playing guessing games? Again, I like to treat others as I wish to be treated, and I would like to know if someone needs something from me. So, whenever we need or want something from someone, *we need to ask!*

When I was a teenager, I used to get really annoyed at my mum because as soon as she walked in the door from work, she started complaining about the mess. She would stomp around the house angrily saying that now *she* had to empty the washing machine, *she* had to do the dishes, *she* had to tidy up – the list went on and on. I used to get annoyed with her for obvious reasons and I used to say, "If you ask me nicely to help Mum, I will help but if you keep moaning, I won't." In hindsight I should have kept my big mouth shut because I was just throwing fuel on the fire.

I was naïve in thinking that she would have asked me for help in a nice manner after my (not so kind) feedback, but if she *had* asked me nicely, I would have helped her. She used to shout back at me saying that I should *know* that the work needs to be done. She was not wrong, but the last thing on my mind as a teenager was keeping the house clean and tidy.

As I talked about earlier, we only see or notice things that we are focused on (like seeing only brown in the colour experiment) and my focus was *not* on a clean house, in fact it was the last thing on my mind. My mother's focus however was keeping a tidy home so she could see the mess but I could only see it when it was pointed out to me.

If my mum wanted me to help her around the house, she just needed to ask. As a mother now, when I feel myself beginning to get annoyed with my kids for not seeing the mess, I smile to myself and remind myself of how I was at that age, and then I ask for help nicely. Nine times out of ten, they are happy to oblige and sometimes they still ignore me but they are human.

No matter who we are, what age we are, whether we are parents, teenagers or middle-aged we all act out and have tantrums from time to time. Sometimes we cry like babies or have tantrums like toddlers but it is due to us either not being able to understand our needs, or frustration due to not having our needs met.

I talk to my kids a lot because my mum rarely spoke to me about feelings (most likely because her mother did not speak to her about feelings). I tell my kids that when they need something from me, they need to ask me for it, whether it be my time, attention, or a cuddle. They often come up to me and say 'I need a hug Mamma,' or ask if we can watch a film and cuddle up in front of the TV and if I can, I will. I am far from being a perfect mother and I still lose my cool from time to time and have tantrums myself, but I remind myself that perfect doesn't exist and forgive myself, and when I'm wrong, I ask for forgiveness from my family too. Communication is the key to keeping peace in our relationships and we have to actually ask for what we need and also accept what we cannot have.

Fear of Rejection

Why don't we just come out and ask for what we desire, especially when it can affect the direction of our life's path? I believe that it is because we are subconsciously scared of the answer being 'NO'. Until we get a 'no' answer then there is still a possibility of a 'yes' answer. It makes sense to allow us to hold on to hope that our proposal will not be rejected but I would rather try and fail than never to know. But perhaps that's just me.

Someone I know has suffered his whole life because when he was young, he fell in love with a girl but he was too scared to tell her. They were good friends at the time but she met and married someone else and he never got over it. Because of this, he lost control of his life which took him on a downward spiral. He also started drinking a lot and smoking 'marijuana' which led him down further still until he ended up suffering with severe mental health issues, all because of a girl and his fear of asking.

His life could have taken a whole other direction, even if he had asked her out and she said no. At least he would have known how she felt about him. Perhaps she liked him too at the time but now he will never know. If he'd asked and she said yes, they could have dated and maybe even decided that they didn't like each other after all, but because he never asked, he will never know. This poor man now lives in a care home and whenever I see him, he still talks about his regret of never asking the love of his life to go on a date. A whole life was wasted and it all stemmed from his fear and not asking for what he wanted.

We all get rejected at some point in life. Perhaps by a love interest, perhaps by not getting the job we really wanted or even by family members, but we learn and grow from all our disappointments and eventually realise that it was the best thing for us. Life happens to all of us and we learn from our experiences but we must always remember that we are blessed with 'free will' and are free to choose.

The famous line in Shakespeare's play Hamlet "To be or not to be? That is the question" makes us wonder whether it is fate or not, but the reality is we decide, and have to act first before fate comes into play. If we don't ask, we certainly won't get!

Whether we need to ask for a job, support, a date, or even a bank loan to start a business, we should just ask because the worst that could happen is that we can be rejected and humiliated which would not come anywhere close to the pain of living a life full of regret.

So, if in doubt, ASK!

• What can you start asking for, today that you have been putting off asking for due to fear of what the answer may be? (Perhaps to spend time with someone? Perhaps you want to get to know someone? To ask for help with something? To ask for a job? To ask for the money back that you lent to a friend?)

True Friends

"Surround yourself with people that want to see you smile!"

It is said that we become like the five people we spend the most time with, so what does this tell us?

It tells us that we have to choose our friends wisely, and also that we have to be a true friend and good influence in other's lives too. In our teenage years we can often turn to, and are influenced by, our friends more than our parents but we have to ask ourselves: "Who wants the best for *me*?" Yes, friends are vital in life but until we know who our true friends are, we have to be careful who we listen to.

The decisions we make at this age are vitally important while taking the first steps into adulthood and creating a life of our dreams, so we have to make wise choices in all areas of our lives, including the kind of friends we want to have.

Like the three little pigs in the classic children's story, if we want to build a house that can keep out the big bad wolf, to keep ourselves and those we love safe, we need to build a strong house, using strong materials. The same goes for our lives. If we want to keep ourselves safe and be protected from the dangers in life, we need to build strong relationships with reliable and supporting people that can help us with-stand the storms of life. Alternatively, if we choose to build our house with straw or sticks by building relationships with people that we know will not stick around when we really need them, we are then unprepared for the storms or the big bad wolf that will eventually come knocking on our door. Solid friendships are built with love, honesty and trust and we know that they always have our best interests at heart. If we feel we don't have these relationships and constantly need to keep pleasing people, doing things to make them happy without following our own gut feelings, we are building our house with straw. And we all know what happens to the straw house, don't we?

Not all of the people that we love and trust, feel the same way as we do. Personally, I love to see my friends happy and living their dreams whatever it takes. Their happiness makes me feel happy and when they are down, I am upset for them but the reality is that not everyone feels this way about us. Some friends are the first to rush to our side when we are broken and in need of a friend but if we are soaring, shining brightly and high on life, they disappear. These times can be very lonely and confusing (as our houses of straw blow away) and we may be tempted to come down off our high so that our friends don't feel bad, but the truth is that if they really loved us, our happiness would be enough for them.

This doesn't make them bad people, they may want to keep things as they are because of their own insecurities and are perhaps scared of losing us, but we cannot live our lives to please others no matter how much they mean to us. When we are being true to ourselves by being the best versions of ourselves, we are moving in the right direction and building strong foundations.

When I was really unhappy and felt lost, my friends were there by my side giving me advice and holding my hand which I was grateful for, but what I found is that when I felt better again, and started to make something of my life, woosh…they disappeared. The one or two friends that stayed were the true ones that were there to celebrate with me as my happiness made them happy too. It was a strange time for me because half of me wanted to go back to being miserable so I could feel loved again, but the reality was that I needed to love myself more, not be loved by others.

People will come and go in our lives but the one person we have to spend every single day of our lives with is ourselves, so it is absolutely essential that *we* love who we are.

If our friends do not rejoice in our happiness or in our accomplishments then it is not our problem but theirs. If they stay away or don't congratulate us on our wins in life, it tells us something about their insecurities and something about our friendship but it tells us nothing about who we are. We do not have to feel bad or guilty for being happy or successful, it is our birth right. We owe it to ourselves to be the best that we can be even if others don't understand it and we certainly cannot allow them to hold us back. Those that truly care about us will be with us through good times as well as the bad, and they are the bricks that help to hold our house together.

In an ideal world all our friends would want to see us smile and we would want the same for them, but again, we cannot make them happy.

As selfish as it may sound, we are each responsible for our own happiness so we *have* to put our needs first, even mothers.

As a mother myself I had always put my kids first, like lots of mothers do, but because of that, I completely neglected myself and my reason for being, and lost a part of me. I gave all my love, time and attention to my children and left nothing for myself. I was left feeling drained, empty and worth nothing and for a time I was not able to tend to my children the way I wanted to.

So even though we love our friends, we have to think of our happiness, our purpose, our future and the foundations we are building to create an amazing life for ourselves. When we take care of ourselves, we are then able to take better care of those that we love.

When we travel in an aeroplane, before we take off, the flight attendants do a demonstration of the safety procedure in case of an emergency, and they tell us how to use the oxygen masks. They always say we have to put our own masks on first before helping our children or others to put on theirs…but why? This used to puzzle me because as a mother, it is only natural for us to think of our kids first.

Once I realised why, it made perfect sense. If we don't take care of ourselves first, we may run out of oxygen and pass out. Then how useful will we be to our children? They wouldn't know how to put the mask on themselves or how to help us. They'd be left scared and alone not knowing what to do and be in distress. Would we really want to do that to them? Absolutely not, so we have to make sure our masks are on first so we can be of use not only to our children but to anyone else that may need us too.

Taking care of ourselves by making the right choices for *ourselves* instead of pleasing our friends, will ultimately be better for everyone. Those of our friends that are genuinely excited and happy for us, when we are happily living life as our best selves, are those that are our true friends.

Vampire Friends

We all find ourselves in toxic relationships from time to time. They can drain our energy and cultivate negativity that leaves us feeling like we've had the life sucked out of us, hence the name 'Vampire Friends'.

Because we become like the people we spend the most time with, we must limit the time we spend with people that drain the excitement and enthusiasm out of us.

We reluctantly hang on to them through a sense of duty, guilt, or just to be a good person but our internal intuition is screaming at us to stay away. But again, we have to put our oxygen masks on ourselves first for everyone's sake. Some people enter into our lives that seemed right at the time but we naturally outgrow them if they choose not to grow with us. Just like all things in life, we have to keep moving in order to get anywhere but if we don't let go of these relationships, they can weigh us down and hold us back. If we don't limit our time with them, there's a chance that we too will become infected with their negativity.

Have you ever sat with friends and listened to them constantly complaining or judging others and then found yourself agreeing or even doing the same? Negativity *is* infectious and it can easily be caught, but we have to keep our minds and souls nourished with positivity and light.

We risk becoming like them, but they can equally become like us, so we have to be an example of light to them, and show them how to shine by shining ourselves. We can't change people but we can inspire them to be brighter and happier souls.

Remember we can choose to either be a 'sunflower', a strong, beautiful and nourishing source of nature, or a 'weed' that sucks the nutrients from the earth, robs good plants from nourishment and strangles the life out of them.

What do you choose to be?

What Kind of Friend Are We?

To grow in life and to improve the quality of our lives we need to first understand who we are in all areas. If we desire to be surrounded with people that lift us and brighten our days, we have to also ask ourselves if we are being that way for others.

1. List all the characteristics/attributes that you would love to see in a true friend (the more detailed the better).
For example: funny, honest, kind, fun, easy to talk to, open, etc.

a.
b.
c.
d.
e.
f.
g.
h.
i.
j.

2. List all of *your* best qualities as a true friend. (For example: I am caring, I make time for my friends, I support my friends.)

a.
b.
c.
d.
e.
f.
g.
h.
i.
j.

3. On a scale of 1–10, How close am I to being the kind of friend that I desire to have in my life? 1 Being I'm nowhere near being the kind of friend I'd like to have, 10 being I'd absolutely love to have myself as a friend.

4. What kind of friend would I describe myself as?

5. How do I want my true friends to treat me?

6. How can I be a better friend to others?

7. What kind of life do I wish for my friends?

We reap what we sow in life, so the kinder and more loving we are, the more loving kindness we will receive.

Self-Confidence

Confidence is something we build, not something we have.

Being confident and having high self-esteem (knowing our worth) do not always come hand in hand. A person can be confident yet still lack self-esteem and a person can know their worth yet still lack confidence.

Just because we know we are of worth as a human being, we can still lack confidence in our ability to do certain things. But the good news is that we can attain both if we want them. We learned earlier in the book about realising our self-worth but how do we build confidence?

We perhaps look at others and say to ourselves, '*I wish I had their confidence*' but we have no idea what they had to do to gain that level of confidence, or if they have it in all areas of life, but I believe that confidence is built through hard work and consistently living up to our own standards, whether it means working on developing our passions and talents, or working on our growth as human beings.

For example, my 18-year-old nephew Joey is a talented singer and guitar player. It is his passion and every chance he gets, he plays and sings, striving to be his best. The minute he steps on to any stage, it is evident that he loves performing because he comes alive. He oozes self-confidence. The bigger the audience is, the happier he is, but when he is offstage and not performing, he goes back to being an average teenager. Joey the performer is super confident but being just Joey is another matter and I think that is the same with a lot of people.

I was the same when I had my hair salon. The minute I unlocked the salon door I was full of confidence because I was sure of my ability as a hairstylist and business owner and my confidence was evident in my work, but outside of work, I was back to being shy and insecure of me, Nadia Wong the human being. I loved my work but I didn't love 'me' quite so much.

When we start off in life, we have big dreams of being the best in our chosen field whether we dream of being a singer, doctor, chef, designer, teacher or whatever we choose to be. And let's face it we all want to be recognised for being great, but what we actually want is to be significant in this world. Every single one of us want to know and feel we are of worth, to know we are meant to be, and know that we are loved.

Some people have greater drive and determination but only when they become a success do they feel significant through their work. When they are doing well, they are happy but when things are not so good, they can lose their confidence. Others give up on their dreams really quickly when they realise how much hard work and resilience it takes, and start to lose confidence, feel worthless and feel powerless over their lives.

Ultimately what all of us crave as human beings is to be significant and to be loved and valued but we have to realise we all have the power within us to create all these things.

This is what I teach in this book. It is not a one-time thing, a one-off exam and if we pass, we are qualified for life. It is creating a growth mindset which means we learn to grow from every experience good and bad, and to face life with courage and faith in ourselves. Every single one of us have to *live* these teachings, not just know them, me included. We need to grow constantly throughout our lives, be grateful for every single day and not waste a single one. We do not know if it will be our last.

I had the great pleasure of meeting Helen an incredible woman that was 99 years old. She was one of the most beautiful human beings I have ever met in my life. I will always value the short time I spent with her. When I asked her what her secret was to living a happy life she said 'learning'. She said that even at 99, she still reads and learns new things every day to keep growing and improving.

She had a beautiful spirit and had a glorious light beaming through her eyes. She was a living proof that beauty does not depend on how we look on the outside. I was not looking at what she was wearing, what her body shape was or examining her hair and face, all I could see was her true beauty shining from her soul. She was an amazing example of a human being that made a significant impact on the lives of others, and mine too.

We can all find a way of being significant to the world whether it's through our work, our behaviour, the way we love, the way we dress, the way we wear our hair, the way our bodies look, tattoos etc. but do we feel significant within? I am all for freedom of self-expression as we have to be true to ourselves but are we using these things to hide who we really are or as a way to feel significant? Do we act and look the way we do to express our true selves or as a cover for our external world to see?

For example, if you knew that nobody would, or could ever see a tattoo that you want, would you still have it done? Do we do what we do, and look the way we look, to feel and look our best for ourselves, or for others to look admiringly at us?

I cannot answer this question for you, only you can, but I can tell you this: From my life experiences, we can only be happy and confident with ourselves when we know we are doing what is right and good in our eyes by being true to ourselves. Referring back to our guiding principles will help us to make choices and build both self-worth and self-confidence. When we live in alignment with who we are regardless of what others think, we can be confident in everything we do, in what we wear, what we say, how we look and so forth. It took me a long time to be free to be myself and to love me for just being me, as I was always worried that others wouldn't like me, but now that I like me, it doesn't matter one bit to me. I know who I am, what is in my heart, what my intentions are in all this work that I do in helping people to use their personal power, and I like who I am.

I am confident because I believe in my work as an author, teacher and coach. I also know I am a worthy human being because I have taken this journey before you to know who I am. I also know that I am no better than anyone else and that nobody is better than me. We are all equal in the eyes of our Creator and no matter what we look like, what we achieve or how successful we are, we are all of great worth. What I teach is not to make you feel better than others but to give you direction in realising your power over yourself and your life to create your own happiness, and to get the most from the precious gift of life. We have all been blessed with all the tools to create a masterpiece of our lives, but we choose whether or not to use them. We can build an abundant life filled with all of life's riches, or just sit back and let life happen to us with no effort on our part.

We can spend our whole lives in search of happiness, but happiness is not a destination, it is a journey of progress as we become better. We often think that when we achieve something, we will be happy and confident. For example, when we are rich, when we lose weight, when we get our book published, when we get married, when we get a promotion, when we have children, when we are famous. We think that *then* we will be happy but happiness is a state of mind and heart of being content with the progress that we are making while living life with love and purpose.

I like to think of life as a happiness train. We can get on at any time and keep moving forward growing every day, or we can get off and stay wherever we are. The train has no permanent stop and the journey continues through our whole lives. The final destination will be the end of our journey on this earth. Now is our time, and we have to live it right here, right now. The only thing we have to do is to decide whether to get on the train and move, or stay at the station and watch the happy train go by.

So many famous talented people turn to drugs and also sadly take their own lives because they are unhappy. They strive to become significant in this world thinking they will feel fulfilled and loved when they are rich and famous but when they get to the top, they realise that they failed to fill the emptiness within them by learning to love and value themselves as human beings. Self-worth and self-confidence are earned through learning to know and value our true selves, through hard work and consistent practise in developing not only our gifts and talents to brighten this world, but by nourishing and developing our souls.

We also have to step outside of our comfort zone and do things that scare us knowing that it will help us to grow and learn. Every time we do something new that we are not proficient at can cause us some anxiety and we can be fearful, but if we continue doing it over and over, we can become confident at it and feel confident within ourselves.

I still get nervous and get scared as I grow further and step out of my comfort zone, but I feel the fear and do it anyway and don't allow my fear to control me, which builds my confidence.

Fake Confidence

The reason some people love alcohol so much is because of the way it makes them feel. They feel a sense of freedom and more relaxed but the trouble is that the feeling of 'fake confidence' is addictive and unsustainable. Meaning they can't drink alcohol all the time to feel free.

Alcohol is not only a temporary fix; it also robs us of our common sense and intellect. The story of the poor young man who wiped out a family because of drinking and driving, as I talked about earlier, demonstrates the real dangers that can be a consequence of drinking. This was a nice boy that simply made a decision to drink, lost all sense of reasoning and decided to take his parents car for a spin. He not only lost his common sense but ultimately, he lost a bright and carefree future, his freedom, his inner peace, his self-worth and has to live with the consequences because of one bad decision. He will now have to spend his entire life with the death of a mother and her two children on his conscience.

Yes, drinking with friends can be fun. Yes, we can have a laugh, but we cannot predict our level of stupidity or how it will end. Our behaviour and the bad choices that we make may only last an evening but the consequences of it may stay with us our entire lives. When under the influence, will we have the common sense to steer clear of drugs and people that will harm us?

I'm 100% sure that the 17-year-old drunk driver had no intentions of harming anyone when he had a drink, never mind taking three lives.

I know how destructive it can be myself because everything that I have ever done, that I have regretted; I did while I was under the influence of alcohol. When intoxicated we do things that we know are not good for us or anyone, and we lose all sense of reasoning and safety. We make poor choices and get ourselves into situations that we can't get out of, but we have to live with the consequences of these events our whole lives. We cannot erase them or go back and change them. The memories are tucked away in that little library of our minds forever.

When drunk we don't just stop caring what others think of us, we stop caring about anything. That to me is not freedom, it's a gateway to lack of awareness and empathy for the world around us, and a road to self-loathing.

Even though I only used to drink on special occasions because of my health, I gave up alcohol altogether many years ago for many reasons, not only because it is unhealthy, ageing on the body, full of unneeded calories and sugar but also because it made me feel bad on so many levels. It made me wheezy for one, I hated hangovers and I always felt regret afterwards. Even if I had only three drinks, my body would let me know it was not happy with me and I suffered a lot so I wondered why I keep putting myself through that. I didn't even like the taste that much. Even though I felt bad physically, the main reason that I cut out alcohol all together was due to the emotions that I felt the morning after, and for some time after. I felt guilty for harming my body, I felt bad for saying things to people that I would never have said otherwise, I felt bad for laughing at people's misfortune and for gossiping with my friends. I hated myself when I drank because I knew I wasn't being the best version of me. Alcohol didn't give me confidence and freedom or make me happy, ultimately it made me stupid and thoughtless.

Now I'm not saying that alcohol is the root of all evil but we have to make sure that if we are drinking, we do so consciously and safely with the right people, and for the right reasons. If we drink to fit in, to be cool, to feel free, then the solution is not alcohol.

The only way to be free is to create that self-worth and self-confidence within ourselves, to love who we are, and to make life better not only for ourselves but for whoever is within our reach.

Whenever I am at parties, I am always the first on the dance floor and the last to sit down at the end of the night. I don't need stimulants to have a good time, and be free, I am high on life and live in the moment.

Instead of trying to fit in with everyone else I dare to stand alone in my soberness, be true to myself by treating myself and my body with the love and kindness I deserve. Some people criticise or judge me for my decision to not drink but nine times out of ten people ask me how I manage to get so much energy and aliveness because they want it too!

1. On a scale of 1–10 How much self-confidence do you have in:
    a.   Yourself as a human being?
    b.   Your work, craft or passion?

2. What level would you like to be in each of these and why?

3. What good reasons would you have for getting drunk with your friends?

4. What good reasons do you have for NOT getting drunk with your friends?

5. Describe how you would look and feel if you were confident?

6. Describe how you would act and behave if you were confident? (how you talk, walk, treat people)

7. Describe how successful you would be if you were self-confident? (what could you achieve?)

8. What is stopping you from being confident now?

9. What can you do to become more confident within yourself?

10. This last one is a task. Dress as though you are confident and going for an interview for your dream job. And walk around as if you are sure they will love you and give you the job.

Now answer this: What areas of your life do you need to develop more to give yourself the best chance of getting the dream job or the dream lifestyle that you desire? (your mindset, your talent, your education)

Love Lesson #5
My Body

"Good Health is True Wealth."

The first thing we have to understand is the value of the bodies that we have. Without these beautiful creations that house our souls, we would not, and could not, be here so we have to realise their worth.

Those of us that are fortunate enough to have full functioning bodies need to realise how truly blessed we are. One of my friends has been living with Multiple Sclerosis for over twenty years and has to use a wheelchair to get around and she gets so frustrated when she sees people 'choosing' to laze around and not enjoy the gift of good working legs. I've heard her say: "If they only knew what they had. I would do anything to have their legs and they aren't even using them!"

Being able-bodied myself, I hadn't even thought of how grateful I am for my legs until she said it. Even though I nearly lost my life due to chronic asthma, I hadn't realised how truly blessed I am to have working limbs.

Colin, one of my old school friends, was a fit and healthy teenager and a great football player but on the way home from a match one day, he and his friends got into a car accident. He was thrown from the car and his body was so damaged that he has spent the last 30 years in a wheelchair. My heart breaks for him as I remember how active and lively he used to be. He needs full-time care and can't eat or drink without help but he is not brain damaged. Even though it isn't easy to understand him when he speaks, he is still a cheeky blighter from time to time and makes me laugh, but life is understandably really hard for him. When we went out for coffee one day, we got onto the subject of worth and he turned to me and said that there was no point to his life. I just wanted to cry for him as I could feel his frustration but I can never know what he has had to endure for all these years. My friend has no choice and can do very little to change his physical body but those of us that are fortunate enough to have working bodies, must make the most of what we have and not waste this precious gift.

When I was in my twenties, I went on holiday to Tenerife with my 'then future

106

husband', and spent 12 of the 14 days lying in a hospital bed fighting for my life. It was truly scary being in a foreign country and being rushed away in an ambulance.

Before then, I hadn't really taken my ill health seriously, I was a young, successful businesswoman and asthma wasn't that serious, was it? I was more concerned that I was not overweight than about whether I could manage my asthma with inhalers and steroids or not. I hadn't really thought that I could do much about my health except stopping smoking which I had already done. So, I labelled myself as an asthmatic and just carried on. On this occasion, however, my inhalers were not working and for two days, I was struggling to breathe. I had experienced this before but not usually this bad. I remember being in our hotel room (because I didn't have the breath to go out) and reluctantly calling the doctor out to see me, at the same time thinking I didn't want to cause a fuss and embarrass myself, but as soon as he saw me, he rushed me off to hospital. I had never been in hospital in my life before, so I was terrified. They pumped me full of drugs, put tubes up my nose and put me on an intravenous drip (and I hated needles). What the heck was going on? I only had an asthma attack. When the doctor came around to see me later, he said that the oxygen in my blood was so low that if I had waited another few hours before calling, I would have died. Even though I was in hospital, I was not out of danger and I could see the seriousness of how ill I was on the doctor's face when he told me that he would do everything he can, but things were not looking good. He had tried everything to get my oxygen levels up but they were not shifting. I was so weak that I couldn't even walk to the bathroom without help.

After 12 days in hospital, the day I was due to fly home, the doctor didn't want to release me as my oxygen levels were not back to normal yet. I was crying as I really wanted to get home to my mum (My mum wanted to fly out to be with me but I didn't want her to worry so I played it down but in hindsight I should have let her come. She would have been worried sick). Anyway, the doctor finally released me, well he had to as I was not his prisoner, but he made me promise that I would go straight to the doctors as soon as I got back, and I did. Even though that was one of the scariest experiences of my life, I am so grateful for it, as it taught me the value of my life, my body and my health. From that moment on, my health has always come above 'everything else' because if I am not here, there is 'nothing else'.

Once I realised how valuable my body and my health was, I made a determined decision to do everything within my power to get my health back on track, and the transformation began. I was already learning about the effects of food and health as my boyfriend had just begun studying Chinese Medicine, but I wasn't really committed. This experience changed everything though, and now I was ready to commit to being healthy and strong again. I became the guinea pig for my boyfriend, overcame my phobia for needles and was his first client. He was driven with a determination for me to be well and we grew in knowledge together. I had no interest in acupuncture and Chinese herbs but I was obsessed with learning about how foods can either harm or heal our bodies. I completely changed my diet and lifestyle and the journey began to not just being better with asthma but to creating a life of abundant health.

Twenty-five years have passed and now my husband is an experienced Chinese Medicine Practitioner and I have learned so much from him. I feed myself and my family a diet of whole, fresh and organic (when possible) foods and don't eat any sugar or processed foods. I am a living proof that we can change our lives and health for the better if we change our lifestyles and create good habits. I haven't taken even a paracetamol for over 20 years. It took some time to be completely medicine-free and to turn my health around but every day took me a step closer to my goal. Don't get me wrong, I will always have that weakness in my lungs and I have to always be careful with what I eat but I am in control of my health now and it doesn't control me. I still carry an inhaler with me but I never use it and my health still always comes first.

We Are What We Eat

We are literally what we eat! We are each made up of all the foods that we have ever eaten and those foods have built these vessels that we live in. Some of us have always been fed good wholesome foods and some not, but we can usually tell which ones have and which ones haven't by the shapes of our bodies, by our energy levels, and by the condition of our skin and health. But please remember that thin does not mean healthy. They are two different things and absolutely cannot be compared.

Because our bodies continually regenerate, we can choose from today on if we want to keep our body and health as it is today, or to start to create a better and healthier version of it.

Imagine if we received a gift of a brand-new car when we were born. A beautiful perfect vehicle, that we arrived in, that could last up to 100 or so years (bearing in mind that not everyone has been given this gift).

Until we are old enough it's our parents' job to take care of our car and as we get older, we start to take care of it for ourselves. During that time, we watch and learn from our parents, and others, about what we need to keep it in optimal working order to get the most out of it now, and also in the future. All it needs is good, clean, high-quality fuel that allows it to run at its best, regular oil checks and changes when needed, and to keep the mechanics in check through regular movement to keep it running smoothly and not seize up. We will only ever have one car in our whole lives but if it is well taken care of, it can last as long as we need it for and keep it looking beautiful.

We may need to renew some parts as it gets old but generally, we are free to use this car throughout our whole lives to give us the freedom to move freely through life, to see the world and to enjoy the physical aspects of life.

If you had the gift of this perfect vehicle, how would you treat it?

- Would you take care of it so it will last a lifetime?
- Would you take it on crazy dangerous roads and hope that it won't get damaged?
- Would you keep it well fuelled with clean good quality fuel to maintain its high quality?
- Would you keep it out of harm's way and treat it with respect?
- Would you let others take control of it and do what they please with it because you don't want to say no?
- Would you keep it clean inside and out to preserve its beauty and longevity?
- Would you appreciate this invaluable gift you have been given and use it to enjoy life to the full?

- Would you keep the engine in good working order by taking it on regular runs or leave it sitting stagnant and unused and never living up to its full potential?

We often expect our bodies to work at an optimal level even when we are treating them badly. We say things like "We only live once so I'd rather enjoy eating and drinking what I like" or "Life is too short; I could die tomorrow." Yes, any one of us could die tomorrow but we can equally live on into our nineties, and what then?

It's about quality, and giving ourselves the best chance at living a good quality life, which means being aware of what we are fuelling our bodies with.

At this age and stage if you are anything like I was, you are probably more concerned about the way you look than the quality of your health but believe me when I say that when you let go of how you look and concentrate on your health, your weight will not be an issue. Only when we focus on our weight and size does it become an issue. We can weigh ourselves to check in with our weight but DO NOT OBSESS over it. Weight goes up and down depending on the time of the month for girls and also how much liquid we retain so please keep this in mind. I can only tell you what I believe to be true because of what I have learned through Chinese Medicine, my experience of how I healed my body and how I have managed to maintain my weight and lifestyle for over 20 years (even after having two children). My body is far from perfect but remember perfect does not exist so it will always be far from perfect. I am happy knowing that my body allows me to live a happy and active life, full of energy and strength. Exactly what I need it for.

Once we learn to love ourselves and value the bodies that we have, we will do all that it takes to maintain health and vitality. At your age you will not be thinking of longevity but know this, "When you get older, you won't feel older in your mind or heart," it is our body that tells us that we are getting older, so if we look after it when we are young we can continue to live life the way we choose instead of only what our bodies allow us to do. Even though we grow in heart and mind as we age and have families, we still care about how we look and feel. If we take care of ourselves by eating healthily when we are young, it will slow down the ageing process which your future self will thank you for, in fact, love you for. We are all ageing and we can never get this day back again so we have to spend each day wisely by nourishing our bodies, minds and souls with the fuel it needs to live fully. We can never go back and fix the past but we can move forward today facing in the right direction and take action.

I had friends when I was young, and you probably do too, that could eat whatever they wanted and never put on weight and stayed skinny. They would smugly sit stuffing themselves full of chips, chocolate, sweets etc. while the rest of us had to hold back. We would be so jealous of them and think that life just isn't fair but believe me when I say that eating a bad diet catches up with you no matter who you are or what your size is. The more junk you eat, the more toxins you consume and they have an effect on the body in some way. It could be either through ill health, weight gain or premature ageing, or even all three, but there is no lucky escape. We reap what we sow, so if we plant bad quality seeds, we reap bad quality lives. It's a harsh but true reality in all areas of life. We always become what we eat so it's a choice whether we want to be full of vitality or full of junk!

Unfortunately, there are still many people suffering from eating disorders because they define themselves by how they look instead of what is in their hearts but once they learn to love who they are and value who they are as human beings, they will understand the importance of feeding their bodies with good clean fuel in the right quantities to create abundant health and an abundant life. If you start off on the right foot when you are young, then life will be easier to deal with. So, ask yourself whether eating non-nourishing foods on a regular basis now is going to serve you in the future, or harm you.

We all come in different shapes and sizes and we are all unique but we are not what we are on the outside. Our book cover says nothing about what is inside where the true value is, as we learned in love lesson #2. Once we realise our true reason for being is to do with our work upon the earth, what love and gifts we give the world, and nothing to do with how we look, we can let go of trying to look perfect.

What would you rather be known for?

    A. Being a wonderful loving and kind person and be loved for it.
    B. Being an attractive person with a perfect body.

What would you hope someone would say about you?

    A. He/she is incredibly attractive.
    B. What an incredibly kind and thoughtful human being he/she is.

We have a false perception that being attractive makes us happy but look at Marilyn Munroe. She is famous for being one of the world's most beautiful women yet she took her own life. She fed her body with alcohol and drugs because she didn't value herself as a human being. Sadly, another life was wasted due to her lack of self-worth and by feeling unfulfilled in life, even with her beauty, fame and fortune.

Since my kids were really small, I have spoken to them about the importance of healthy living. They used to wonder why everyone else got sweets and chocolate but they were not allowed so I had to explain about health and how we all have choices. I know first-hand how what we eat affects our health so I could not feed my kids something that I myself was not prepared to eat. Healthy living is also one of my guiding principles so I cannot feed *anyone* things that I know could harm them in any way.

To keep it simple for my kids to remember about good health, I used to hold up my hand and they would point to each finger and tell me what living a healthy lifestyle needs.

1. GOOD HEALTHY FOODS
2. WATER
3. FRESH AIR
4. EXERCISE
5. REST

Good Healthy Foods

We all know what we should and shouldn't eat on a day to day basis, so I will not lecture you on the dos and don'ts, but I will give you some guidelines to follow and some important information that helped me to create abundant health in my life.

According to Chinese Medicine and the experience of my incredibly talented husband, we have to eat well-balanced meals including all nutrients. In the world of today, there are hundreds of diets out there that claim to be healthy and now none of us know what is good for us or not, so I will share with you some guidelines that my husband teaches to help his clients to regain health and vitality in life.

My Food Guidelines:

1. Eat clean and natural organic unrefined foods. They will not only nourish our bodies but will minimise the toxins that we consume that are harmful to the body.
2. Carbohydrates are *not* the enemy, but we have to eat whole grains e.g. brown pasta, brown rice etc. instead of white to gain nourishment from them.
3. Limit or eliminate dairy products because we as humans do not have the enzymes to digest the lactose in cow's milk and therefore overwork our digestion and cause dis ease. When our bodies struggle to digest certain foods, our bodies need to work harder, which saps our external energy and leaves us feeling tired and moody.
4. Eat before 7 pm because digestion slows down considerably and therefore, we are unable to breakdown the foods sufficiently
5. Eliminate refined sugar, this is a hard one to swallow (pun intended) but sugar feeds disease in the body so by eliminating it we are optimising our health. It is not only damaging to the teeth from the outside it damages them, and our bones, from within.
6. Limit animal products. Meat and dairy (along with processed foods) are highly acidic and to be healthy we need to eat a diet of primarily alkaline foods which include fresh fruits and vegetables. So, plant-based food is always better.
7. Eat consciously. Personally, I take a few moments to give thanks for the food I eat for two reasons. a.) To remind myself to be grateful that I have good food to eat. b.) To bring me to the present, take a few slow breaths and sit calmly instead of eating without even tasting and enjoying the food.
8. Always eat breakfast, never skip meals and always carry healthy snacks wherever you go so you are not tempted to eat junk when you are out and about and get hungry. For example, dried fruit and nuts, healthy crackers or fruit.
9. Drink very little during meals (Ideally drink at least 20 minutes before eating and 20 minutes after to optimise digestion). This is to optimise digestion without diluting the stomach acids that break down foods. It is also a way to consciously eat slower and chew our foods well, knowing that we can't wash them down.
10. Eat according to the seasons. For example, in summer you can eat raw vegetables such as salads and in winter eat cooked vegetables like soups. If we

eat raw cold foods in the winter it can cause bloating and we can even put on weight due to creating cold and damp inside.

Because of all the fad diets out there we are led to believe that certain foods are not good for us. For example, society says that low carbs or no carbs is best but according to Traditional Chinese Medicine (TCM) we all need carbohydrates as part of a balanced diet. We are also led to believe that protein powder is good for us but is it even real food? These things may help us to lose weight or build muscle but what about our overall health? Looking good does *not* mean we are healthy. The more natural foods we eat, the better they are for us. We can't go too wrong with good real home cooked meals, and they are usually the tastiest too. Real food cooked in the way it was meant to be eaten is absolutely the best way to go.

I am half-Chinese and half-Italian and I practically eat rice and pasta daily, with lots of fresh vegetables and my weight has stayed pretty consistent over the past 25 years due to eating real food and not dieting. The best way to make any life choices is to ask ourselves: 'Will this help me or hurt me?' and our choices are made easy by the answer that follows.

When I was young, we were told that breakfast was the most important meal of the day and I agree. How can we expect to have lots of energy throughout the day without fuel? Would we jump into our cars when there is no fuel and expect them to take us where we need to go? If we use our common sense and treat our bodies with love and respect, we can live healthy and happy lives.

To give you an idea of what a typical day is for me, here are some examples of what I feed myself and my family:

Day 1

- Pre breakfast… Aloe Vera gel or hot water with lemon followed by milk kefir (a probiotic drink that I cultivate at home packed with good bacteria that fights off the bad…like yoghurt but better).
- Breakfast. Overnight oats = Oats soaked overnight (or even an hour) with rice or soya milk, bananas, cacao nibs, coconut, raisins or goji berries, chia seeds and sometimes seasonal fruits added (I also vary the ingredients).
- Lunch… Whole wheat pasta with a fresh tomato sauce and Grana Padano cheese served with salad or vegetables
- Dinner… Boiled brown rice with a runny steamed organic egg with soya sauce, served with salad or veg.

Day 2

- Pre breakfast… Aloe Vera / lemon water and kefir.
- Breakfast… Porridge oats cooked with banana, water and rice/soya milk topped with fruit or naturally sweetened jam.
- Lunch… Brown rice salad with tuna, tomatoes, olives, peppers, lettuce, rocket, sweetcorn, carrot (any other vegetables chopped up really small and mixed in…you can use one or two veggies or all) dressed with olive oil and

apple cider vinegar.

- Dinner… Rice noodles with grilled fish and spinach.

Day 3

- Pre breakfast… Aloe Vera and kefir.
- Breakfast…Naturally sweetened cornflakes with rice/soya milk.
- Lunch… Whole-wheat spaghetti Carbonara (my version) made with courgettes, Parma ham, and an organic egg.
- Dinner… Brown rice with spicy Mexican beans and salad.

I tend to eat fruit as snacks (cooked in the winter) or I make my own naturally sweetened desserts. I also drink green tea after meals and throughout the day. Being Chinese, I grew up drinking it and my dad always used to tell us that it breaks down fat so there was always a pot brewing. Even though green tea only contains a small amount of caffeine, one year I decided to stop drinking it to optimise sleep, but without changing anything in my diet I put on two kilos in weight. I couldn't work out what it was until I started drinking it again and the two kilos disappeared. I drank green tea because I liked it but after my weight increase, I realised that there may be some truth to my dad's wise words.

We are all different shapes and sizes, have varied appetites, and we all use different amounts of energy, so calorie counting just makes us crazy. At your age when you may still be growing it is essential that you eat well. Using the story of the three little pigs again here signifies that if we build strong houses made with good materials, we can withstand the storms when they come and they always come, this is life. The quality of the food that you eat should be high. Instead of focusing on how much you eat you should focus on the kind of foods you are eating. If you have an enormous appetite (like I used to have) fill up on vegetables. If you need to lose weight, eat less and move more. Simple.

There are times when we are more active and need more food, so we have to listen to our bodies, but at the same time always be conscious of *what* we are eating. There are certain times of the month for females when we feel the need to eat more or perhaps something chocolaty and sweet so at the end of this lesson, I will include a few natural sweet treat recipes that will satisfy the taste buds, are healthier options and only take minutes to make.

Water

Water is an absolute must for every single human being and without enough, our bodies cannot function. eight glasses of water a day will keep everything running smoothly, keep us hydrated and keep us clean on the inside. We wouldn't go out without washing ourselves on the outside but what about the inside? Just because we cannot see it, it doesn't mean it doesn't matter.

We don't talk about our poo often enough but it tells us so much about our health. Now I'm not talking about taking a poo sample to the doctors to get analysed, I'm talking about the smell, the colour, the consistency of it and how often we go. I know this isn't fun to talk about (even though it makes me giggle), it is wise to have a basic knowledge of healthy poo.

I remember when my boyfriend was doing his TCM training and I was his guinea pig, I had to go into class with him and his tutor would ask what my stools (poo) were like. I nearly died of embarrassment…but I survived.

You'll be pleased to know that I am not going to give you a description of my stools but I will share with you what I learned.

- We should poo at least once a day. If we don't then we need to increase our water intake, vegetables and fibre.
- Poo should be poo shaped and soft to the touch (only joking about the touch bit, LOL)
- If poo is runny, watery or undigested (with bits in it), then raw foods should be limited until poo is normal again, and make sure you are chewing your food sufficiently.

Sometimes in the winter I struggle to drink eight glasses of water as I actually don't feel thirsty, so I squeeze some fresh organic lemon into a big glass jug, throw in the peel and I sip it throughout the day. I also drink herbal teas or boiled water with lemon to stay hydrated.

Lemon water is good for helping to keep the body alkaline and is said to also aid weight loss so it's a good all-rounder. We can't actually go wrong with it.

Many years ago as a hairstylist and daily swimmer, I learned that to avoid damaging my hair and to protect it from the chlorine in the pool, I had to saturate my hair with clean water first. Hair is like a sponge so filling it with clean water meant that it was already full, and therefore the chlorinated water could do less damage. It makes sense, right?

Well our bodies (and minds) are the same. If we fill them with good clean ingredients first, then less damage can be done by what else follows. If coffee is the first thing we drink, then we are filling our body with a stimulant but if we fill it with water or other cleansing liquids, we are saturating our bodies with goodness.

We are not only what we eat, but we are also what we drink.

Fresh Air

This kind of goes without saying but getting fresh air is absolutely essential to good health and well-being. Being out in nature, breathing clean air, taking in the energy from the earth.

I love walking in nature, in a park, by a river, by the sea and taking the time to look around at the beautiful world we live in. It is not only good for our lungs but for our minds as we use this time away from technology. Whenever we get a minute we switch on our phones, our TVs or our computer screens, but we are becoming detached from the actual beauty of this world and are connecting less with nature and real people. We say that this world has come so far and we are advancing in technology but to be honest I am glad I didn't have all these distractions when I was your age.

Life can be so confusing but it is really important to remember that *you* are in control of your thoughts, your minds, your health, your decisions for life. Technology is only a distraction as I mention earlier in the book and you can choose whether to let it control your life or not. Spending time by yourself thinking and appreciating this wonderful gift of life will open your lungs, your heart and your mind to allow you to be free to just be.

Living here in Italy I am able to go to the beach often during the summer and you should see the number of elderly people that walk in the sea to soothe their legs and to get nourishment from the saltwater. They stand in the sea early in the mornings, before it gets too hot, and chat about how much better they feel when they are in the healing waters of the sea.

This earth has everything that we need to survive and be healthy but we human beings are destroying the planet instead of enjoying the true nature of it.

If you are not used to being out in nature, commit to giving yourself 30 minutes a day to go for a walk in all weathers, no excuses. The more you do it the more you will love the freedom you will feel and the connection with the earth. If you get bored then concentrate on practising gratitude, focussing on what you want to see and set yourself little tasks such as:

- How many different kinds of trees can you count?
- How many different types of flowers can you count?
- What shapes can you see in the formation of the clouds?
- What sounds can you hear?
- How many types of birds can you hear or see?

I used to go for walks with my kids when they were small and we would play 'I spy with my little eye' and we would notice all sorts of things.

Remember that we find what we are looking for, so if we are looking for things to enjoy in nature, we will find them. If we go out with a thought that we will not see any beauty, guess what? You will not see any beauty.

Exercise

Fresh air and exercise actually come hand in hand, and getting exercise out in the open is the healthiest kind of exercise. We can kill two birds with one stone, save time and enjoy doing both simultaneously.

As I mentioned earlier, I love running. Once I realised that I was in control of my body and not the other way around I discovered my real power. Running is my meditation as it allows my mind and heart to be free from stress. It gives me freedom of thought and I am inspired as I run.

Because I had breathing difficulties in the past, I did a breathing course which taught me that asthmatics don't suffer because they don't breathe enough, it's because they over breathe or can't control their breathing, so I learned how to breathe correctly. I was taught to breathe in and out through the nose only, as the nose works as a kind of filter. I was also taught to completely fill my belly with air and to breathe with my diaphragm not the top of my lungs. This does take a bit of practise but is the base of yoga and meditation too which is why both are so beneficial to the body. When I run, I focus on my breathing which is so beneficial for my lungs, my mind and my heart.

I believe that exercise should not be a chore. What do I mean? I mean that it should not be done against our will. Okay, we may need to push ourselves a little to get started and build up momentum but I mean we should do things that lift our soul and things that we love. For example, I love running and walking, and I get upset if I miss a day. I love swimming too and also love dancing and dance around my house whenever I get the chance.

My point is that as long as we actively move doing something that we love, either alone or in a class or group, I believe that we can be healthy. Sitting still lounging about and hardly moving doesn't only have negative effects on our health but also on our mood and happiness levels.

It is common knowledge that movement and exercise increase energy, lifts mood and releases stress, so why don't we move more? Perhaps because our eating habits are not giving us the energy that we need. Poor digestion equates to having low energy so in order to increase energy we need to not only eat well but to keep ourselves moving as much as we can.

Again, when we stop focusing on our weight and our body shape and think of being healthy, we will be happy to move in ways that we love. Our bodies will thank us for it and give us all that we need. I am not a patient person when it comes to exercise and I like to do what I like to do. Of course, we would all love beautifully defined muscles but for me, it is more work than I want to do on myself. It is not my priority and as long as I am a healthy weight and full of energy, that is good for me. My life, my work, my health does not call for well-defined muscles so I am living up to my standards. I may change my mind in the future but I am fine and happy with myself as I am. But you may be different.

While I was watching the movie 'Thor' the other day, I was admiring the actor Chris Hemsworth's body (from a coach's perspective only, of course) and I was thinking about how many hours he has to work-out to get that perfectly defined torso. His career depends on it though and it is a priority for him. He will also have to eat a strict diet no doubt, and can't come in from working on a set all day and sit down with a beer and a packet of crisps, so massive sacrifice, determination, consistency and action has to be made on his part.

It all depends on what we want in life and what is essential for us to be happy with who we are. What is essential however is that we are the best that we can be for us, and not to please anyone else.

I bumped into a friend of mine when I was visiting my home town and she looked incredible. She didn't have a millimetre of fat on her but well-defined lean muscle. I told her how great she looked and I was so surprised at her reply when she said, "Thank you. It takes a *lot* of work!"

How refreshing to hear someone be so honest. I admired her honesty because she didn't make out that it was natural, she had to put in the hours and dedication into shaping her body the way she wanted it to be. She was quite rightly proud of her work. I for one don't have her levels of dedication but as I said that is not one of my priorities.

We are all guilty of comparing ourselves to others but we actually have no idea how much time, energy, effort and sacrifice that others put into their achievements, yet we still compare.

If someone is working hard on themselves whether they are winning sports trophies, excelling at university, climbing up the promotional ladder at work or building a great physical shape, they are reaping what they have previously sown. They put the work in and now they are getting results.

We compare the worst versions of ourselves to most likely the best versions of others, but any comparison is a sure way to diminish our self-worth. So again, don't compare yourself to others. Compare yourself with who you are now, to who you desire to become.

We can each achieve far more than we give ourselves credit for but it is all down to the decisions we make and the action we take!

Rest

We don't need a degree to know that we all need eight hours of sleep and good quality rest in order to be healthy, but we are all so different and need varying amounts of sleep. According to the National Sleep Foundation, teenagers need between 8–10 hours' sleep, and young adults between seven and nine but teenagers are notorious for sleeping late.

When I was a teenager, we had an unusual family routine because my parents had a Chinese restaurant. They would come home from work after midnight with a takeaway of all the leftover foods that needed to be eaten. As soon as I heard the key turning on the front door I used to leap out of bed, run downstairs to see what delicious foods were on the menu. It was nice to have family time but I had no idea how unhealthy it was. If I knew then what I know now, perhaps I would never have struggled with asthma as I was totally clueless. I had no idea that what we eat and when we eat plays such an important role in the quality of our lives and health, which is why I share my stories with you. These days, however, the world is much more informed about health and life which actually makes it more surprising as obesity and other food-related illnesses sweep across the globe…even with all the information that we have.

There are pros and cons for living in the 21st century. Pros being that we can have all the information that we need at the touch of a button but the cons are that we have all the information at the touch of a button. Why? Because in this world of technology we are less attracted to fresh air, exercise, real face-to-face conversations and connections, but also because our mobile devises interrupt our sleep. I know this because when I first got my smart phone, I was on it all the time and I would wake up during the night actually buzzing, and not from excitement. My body would literally be shaking inside and I'd feel full of anxiety. I spoke this through with my husband and he said that he had so many clients that experience the same.

In Traditional Chinese Medicine (TCM), if we do not get enough sleep, the organ systems cannot regenerate sufficiently. My husband advises all his clients to totally switch off their devices at least two hours before bed to improve the quality of sleep and to allow the body's natural healing process to take place.

When we lose sleep, apart from being physically tired, we function at a lower capacity, we are moodier, we have trouble concentrating, and we feel less joy. I remember watching a documentary a few years ago on how sleep patterns affect children's performance at school. They took a group of children and made them go to bed early every night for a week and then took an aptitude test. The following week the same children were given free rein over their bedtime and they stayed up later every night and took the same aptitude test. I was not surprised at all that they performed so much better in the week of early nights.

Again, we don't need studies to know that we ourselves are better, brighter, happier, have more energy and feel more attractive when we get a good night's sleep. So, for that reason alone, we should ensure a good night's sleep...*but* don't overdo it! Waking up early is just as important as getting a good night's sleep.

We can waste our lives sleeping through the day but we can never know if today will be our last so we have to spend it wisely. My near-death experience, which I could have labelled the worst time in my life, turned out to be one of the greatest blessings. If not for that, I perhaps would have spent my whole life struggling and getting by, but here I am alive and full of energy and vitality after turning my life and health around. If I could go back and visit my younger self, I would give her a big hug and say, 'Thank you for loving me enough to give me this life and health.' Your future self will also thank *you* for loving yourself enough to make the changes now.

Sleep is essential in creating a good quality life but if you want to create an abundant and successful life too, sleeping more than you need is *not* the way to go. Again, the quality of our lives comes down to the decisions that we make and the actions we take.

Top tips for a good night's sleep:

- Switch off all devices at least one hour before bed and leave it far from where you sleep, preferably in another room.
- Go to bed early and wake up early
- Read something positive before bed as we will go to bed with a peaceful and positive heart.
- Don't go to bed angry, work on the tips in the section 'Dealing with anger'.
- Don't eat after 7 pm.
- Meditate or Pray for a few minutes to help you to release any tension.
- Write down three things that you are grateful for or what went well in your day.

No matter where you are today, whether you are skinny, a healthy weight or overweight, it is never too late to start. Even if you commit to changing only one small thing out of all the advice I give in this section, then it is a step in the right direction and you will realise the power and strength that you have over your body, and how you look and feel. Nobody is to blame for the past but we are in control of the present and we can act.

Let's say for example you decide to either – not eat after 7 pm – start drinking eight glasses of water a day or – go to bed early only for one week, how do you think that would affect your body? Your well-being? Even if you didn't feel or look better, you will know the gift that you have given yourself by beginning to treat yourself with the love that you deserve.

If you have a long road ahead, then take one small step at a time and eventually you will get there. Just as a baby learns to walk, they take one step, then two, then three and with persistent practise they start walking. Imagine if they took one step and fell over and then said, "Nah, it's too hard. Walking isn't that important. Walking is not for me."

We too have to take baby steps when we make changes in our lives and not try to run before we can walk so commit to doing something today and track your progress so you can see how far you have come.

Tracking

I believe that tracking is such a powerful tool to keep us moving forward in the right direction in all areas. Well, it has certainly helped me. What do I mean by tracking? Tracking is keeping a note on paper or in digital form, from where you have come, to where you are going. Let me give you an example. When I started running, I used to walk a little and run a little and did so consistently, running more and more each time until I could run 3 km as I talked about earlier, but once I reached my goal of running 3 km I thought, *what now?* I didn't want to overdo the running because I didn't want to damage or wear out my joints (well I was 45 when I started), so instead of running more each time, I decided to set myself a goal of running 365km from the 1st of January. In order to know how far I run I needed to track my progress, so every time I ran 3 km, I wrote it down. Somehow watching those numbers rise each week gave me the motivation to keep going. I had only just learned to run and did wonder if I'd set myself too big a goal but as the numbers crept up, it made me more determined and I wanted to run more and more just to see the progress I was making. I felt amazing because not only had I mastered running, which I had previously told myself that I could never do, I was reaching my goal. By the end of that first year I ran 410 km…and I was ecstatic! I was so proud of myself for achieving and surpassing my goal and it was another solid confirmation for me that we can do anything if we want it enough.

I would have run from time to time but I am 100% sure that if I had not tracked my progress, I would not have achieved what I did. It gave me the drive I needed to run when I was tired, to run when it was raining, to make time when I had none.

Brownies, Girl Guides and Scouts do certain activities to earn badges, that they wear proudly, as a way to track their achievements and progress. It proves that they are progressing and helps them to build confidence and know they are growing in knowledge and ability.

Progress and growth is what makes us happy. Happiness is not a destination it is a state of mind and heart and if we are progressing and growing in our lives and in ourselves, we feel good, if we are not, we don't. That simple. Have you ever achieved something that you were not sure you could do but you did it anyway? I've done it on many occasions. Getting my health in order, working my way out of depression, running and also writing. I now know that the only way to truly fail is never to try. All that I do and progress in, has allowed me to create a state of happiness. I have failed at lots of things too but from each failure I learned something. For example, before I became a life coach and writer, I started a network marketing business which I totally failed at. I loved it because I believed that I could make a difference to people's lives but it was not for me. After spending a lot of money and two years working consistently, I still failed. But that time in network marketing taught me so much. It helped me to see my true path and helped me to shape my future. I was not getting anywhere in business but I was still progressing as it opened my eyes to another side of life. Okay my business failed but I still grew. If I could go back and change any part of my life, I would not do it because it got me to where I am. If I had not felt unloved as a child, if I had not had asthma and nearly died, if I had not suffered with depression, I would not be the person I am today. So, whatever you are facing, or will face in life, you can grow from. Everything that happens, happens for a reason to shape you into who you are meant to be. Yes, it takes work. Yes, it takes time. Yes, it takes consistency and resilience, but as you continually make progress and achieve what you want in life, that is where true happiness blossoms.

Labels

What is it about labels that drive us all crazy? We have a fascination and fixation of labelling *everything* and *everyone* (including ourselves), but doing so is stunting our growth as individuals as well as a race. Labels can stop us from being free to be ourselves if we allow them to, and force us to follow trends and fads instead of looking within. Why can't we just be who we are with no labels and why do we feel this need to fit into a certain category instead of just 'being'?

The reality is that when we label items, we can keep them in order and when we need something we know where to find them. But when it comes to people, labelling doesn't work.

From a really young age, I was very organised. Mess and confusion upset me and I felt irritated when things were not in their place and I could not find them. My mum loved me for this as she never had to tell me to tidy my room as it was the most clean and tidy room in the house. As soon as I started earning money, I didn't waste it buying frivolous things. I had plans. I designed a 'built-in wardrobe' and had it made for my bedroom with mirrored doors so that there was no mess to be seen and to make my room feel bigger. It cost me over £1,000 which was a massive amount of money in 1989 but for me it was essential.

Within that wardrobe I had box sections built-in and I labelled each box and section, literally. Trousers, jumpers, underwear, make-up etc. It was amazing and I loved it but the problem was when I got a new item that didn't quite fit into any of the boxes, I got really frustrated. I would leave it in a pile somewhere else until I would work out where to put it but each odd item I had, would never have a place. I then began to have a pile of misfits. These misfits were my favourite items because they were different but ended up in a heap in the corner because there was no place for them.

My point is, are we doing the very same to ourselves? We are all diverse and unique and don't always fit into society's boxes but because we do not fit in, we try to shape ourselves to fit in. We go outside of who we truly are so that we can be like others. We compromise our guiding principles and what we believe in, to fit into a certain box. When we do this however, we conform to society and if we don't escape, that is where we tend to remain, in our place.

When I was young when someone was, what we labelled as, 'overconfident', people used to say, "He needs to be put in his place," so we used to fear being outstanding or brilliant. Normal was the place to be. But honestly, who wants to just be normal? I know I used to. Because of being mixed race, I wanted to be normal but normal is where we exist without truly living and where lack of self-worth grows. In this box of normality, we stop growing and start to feel trapped, and desire to be significant. Subsequently, we usually decide to change our labels and put our self in a different box, but if we really want to stand out and be a light, we have to remove the labels and stop allowing ourselves to be put into any box. We all label ourselves in all areas of our lives but once we let go of these labels, we can be free to be our true selves. If we do however need to label ourselves, let's be like Girl Guides or Scouts and fill our sleeves with badges of achievements due to our growth and influence.

How do we label ourselves?

When we use labels when it comes to our health, looks or body shape we tell ourselves that that is who we are and define ourselves. For example, perhaps I would label myself as "a health nut at a healthy weight and shape". But if others were to describe me, they would say something different depending on their point of view. I don't mean their opinion. I mean their actual point of view. Let me explain: If a person is overweight, they would say I was skinny or slim, but if they were skinny, they would say I was shapely and healthy. Very few people would say I was fat because the reality is that I am not fat. I have fat, but I'm not fat. I used to label myself as fat and ugly and I was slimmer than I am now, but that was due to me not being my own best friend. Once I decided that I deserved to be treated with more kindness by others, I also had to start being kinder to myself. It took me a long time to stop calling myself ugly as it had become a bad habit, but I managed to break it. Sometimes even now when I have a bad day, I hear the 'U' word slip from my tongue but I apologise and say out loud 'Sorry Nadia, you are not ugly, you are beautiful'. Sounds crazy right? But if I treat myself badly then I am setting the standard of how I want to be treated.

Another example is that of height. I am also an average height but those who are smaller than me describe me as tall, and those taller than me describe me as small. So, labels are not accurate readings of who we are, what we look like, or how successful we are. It all depends on the point of perception. When we are told often enough that we are ugly or stupid then we start to believe it. I have had experience of this first hand and I was convinced that I was what a certain person continually told me that I was. It was only when I started to build confidence and start to love myself that I realised that their perception of me was not accurate.

We wrongly use other people as mirrors in which to see ourselves, but in actual fact they are like the fun mirrors that are at fairs and amusement parks that transform us. We find this amusing because we know exactly what we look like as we have real mirrors at home but if someone had never seen themselves before, they would believe that the image looking back at them was a true reflection. The only way to know who we really are is to look within. When we know and love ourselves and someone tells us something different, we know we are looking at distorted reflections of us.

What kinds of labelling are there? There are countless but let us discuss a few that are relevant to us today.

Clothes labels to differentiate size
Designer versus high street clothing labels
Personality labels
Achievements and qualifications
Health and wellness

Clothes' labels to differentiate size.

I literally cut the labels out of all my clothes because they irritate my skin (it is the thread that they use to make them that annoys me) but I also think that I have some kind of psychological dislike to them and my body naturally rejects them. Yes, I know I'm weird (label), but let me tell you what I mean. Well, I have already explained my dislike for labels but when it comes to the size of our clothes, they too hold us back from being our best but why?

I love clothes and like to look as 'pretty' as I can. It's part of who I am naturally. I was the same when I was a little girl and nothing much has changed. When I was around nine years old there was a fire on the top floor of our three-storey house. My big sister came running down the stairs screaming, and everyone was in a panic. Because I was on the second floor, I didn't actually see the fire so I quickly got dressed into a pink dress, brushed my hair, ran downstairs, out the door and into the garden where my sisters were standing in their underwear. There I stood all pretty and presentable and my sisters looked like…well, like people that had ran out of a house on fire.

So, looking presentable is just part of me but I have my pet hates when it comes to clothes. I hate tight clothes that restrict my comfort and I don't do casual. I just don't feel like myself. The problem with this is that comfortable clothes are usually casual so I always have to buy bigger sizes for certain clothes. I have always done this and I would *never* buy anything without trying on at least two different sizes. I tend to hold things up to my body and judge whether it would fit me or not, then take it to the changing room along with a size bigger just in case. All clothes are sized differently depending on the item, the fabric and the style so if I was to say I was a size ten and it didn't fit I would buy whatever size fits. Now I know this is normal, but what a lot of people tend to do is to label themselves as a size and then stick to it regardless how it looks or feels on the body. In order to be a size X, they squeeze their butt into that size, and feel pleased with themselves. In doing this however there can be problems:

- The clothes are uncomfortable.
- Any excess skin has to go somewhere and it usually hangs over.
- They restrict movement and circulation.
- They make you look fat even if you are not fat.
- They make you feel fat even if you are not.

If we let go of the restrictions that labels put on us, we will feel better, look better and not have to feel 'not good enough'. If someone was to make an outfit for you, they would take your measurements and make it to fit your form. That simple. They wouldn't ask what size you are and make you an outfit would they?

It's actually not the labels that are bad, it's the meanings that *we* attach to them that harm us. So, don't buy clothes that have your size written on the label, buy what looks best on you, feels best on you and makes you feel amazing. If it doesn't, don't buy it.

As I was pondering over this subject, I was thinking about how similar this is to life and how we try to squeeze our butts into a label hoping to be labelled as another kind of character and not our true form, we may feel:

- Uncomfortable and trapped in a role or title.
- Our true self cannot be tucked away and our true self will spill out some-where
- It restricts our freedom and movement in being ourselves.
- We look unhappy
- We feel unhappy

Therefore, we have to create a life that looks good and feels good on us, without trying to squeeze into a label, size or shape that society has provided for us. We simply have to be ourselves.

Designer versus high street labels

This is a whole other discussion but an equally important one. So many of us are fixated on having certain labels of shoes, bags and clothes, and we all feel pressured into buying them, but at what cost? We feel under pressure to work more and earn more money trying to keep up with the trends but it is never enough. There is always some new and updated version of what we have, so not long after we have what we want, it becomes dated and not good enough. We become a victim to trends, and get sucked into a world of becoming followers instead of leaders. If some people cannot afford this kind of life and don't have the means, they either get themselves into debt in order to keep up, or feel like they are failing, so why do we do it?

- So we can look like we have money?
- So we can feel good about the fact we are wearing labels?
- So we can fit in with everyone else?
- So we don't feel like we are less than others?
- So we feel good enough?
- So we can stand out and feel better than others?
- So we can gain social status?

Families are falling apart as parents are working more and more and have very limited one to one time with each other, and with their kids. Obtaining material items doesn't just add more financial pressure to our lives, it affects the peace and harmony within our families. Is that a price we are willing to pay?

Now I am not saying designer or high-end brands are bad by any means but we have to really ask ourselves why we need to have the latest models. Is it because the quality is so good that it will last longer and save us money in the end? Or is it because everyone else has it and we want it too? What we need to question is *why* we want it and consider the price (not in money) that has to be paid. If we know why we really want something, then we must be prepared to work for it, and then the reward will be great because we know how much it is worth. Only then can we wear it with pride.

My point is that if we learn to appreciate what we do have and be grateful for even the simple things, then we will be happy. Trying to keep up with the world to be as good as, or better than others is like looking for the pot of gold at the end of the rainbow. Trying to be significant through the labels that we wear and to make us look good, and feel good is a waste of time because the only way to feel significant in the world is through what we *give* and who we *are*, not what we wear or the material items that we obtain. The truth is that it will make us feel fantastic for a brief moment as we show off our labels but true worth has to come from within not from how we look, what our bodies are like or what we wear.

Personality labels

We have already talked about this in love lesson #1, about who we are and who we want to become, but when we label ourselves as people and personality types, we are still restricting our growth as human beings. We can use words to describe us partially but only we truly know who we are and we cannot clearly put it into words or put a label on it. We are who we are. It's fine to describe ourselves, our personality, our attributes, our sentiments but there is only one unique being such as ourselves. Every day we grow and progress so we cannot be stamped as this or that. We are lots of things and there is no limit to how much we can grow emotionally, intellectually or spiritually.

When we meet new people we often get asked "What do you do?" but how often do we get asked the question "Who are you?" You see we are all equal and whether we are a domestic worker or the Prime Minister, our worth is based on who we are and what we give, not what we do for a living. It is not our place to judge anyone no matter what they do, or don't do, but we have to be the keeper of ourselves. Labels do not define people, it's the way they love and the way they treat people that determines their value as a human being. Those that love fully and openly do not need recognition or to be labelled as a good person to feel good about themselves, they feel good for being the people they are. That is the true reward.

Over the years I have tried on occasion to start writing a book but as I got a few pages in, I went blank. I've always had this feeling that I would write a book but it seemed so far-fetched and so beyond my capabilities. I was never that clever at school. I got by, but I had no interest in becoming an academic. Because of that I had labelled myself as incapable. I had a 'desire' but fear and doubt in my ability always stopped me. I had labelled myself as not good enough or not capable. 'I' did that, no one else. If I had held on to that label, I would not be doing what I am doing. We choose the labels that we wear and we can also change them.

In the Collins English Dictionary, the word 'Author' means:

1.   *a person who writes a book, article or other written work*
2.   *an originator or creator.*

This is what I do, but I do not label myself as an author because in my mind I will only be an author when my books are published, which as I write this, I am not... YET! I write books (this is my second) and I know they are of great value because otherwise I wouldn't be writing them. Yet, I still wait for the stamp of 'author' which changes absolutely nothing. I have a strong mindset and a determined spirit which I have spent time developing and I write with pure joy in my heart as I share what I have learnt over the years. I believe that this book will be a valuable guide for others through life and to set them in the right direction. If I sell one copy or millions, nothing changes. I am who I am and I love sharing what I have learned in my life. I have a wholehearted desire to help every one of my readers to understand who they are and to help them to grow love in their hearts for themselves and for others. I do not need a label to tell me who I am. I know. I am me and I make no excuses for it because my intentions are pure and all I do, I do with love and for love, not for money.

We choose the labels that we wear, whether they help us or hold us back, and we choose who we are. We can choose to be good, kind, loving, caring people and wear our labels with pride and joy, or choose to be "not good enough, not clever enough, not strong enough". Whatever we decide to be, we will become, so if you are wearing labels that hold you back, tear them off and replace them with ones of courage, determination and love.

Achievements and qualifications

We also use our achievements and qualifications as labels but they too are not always accurate. Just because we have completed a course or memorised facts and materials, and passed our exams, doesn't mean we will do a good job or be good at what we do. What really matters is what is in our hearts and how we use the information that we have gathered. It's about learning with our hearts and not with our minds. It's about becoming passionate about what we do that qualifies us to wear the labels that are handed to us in the form of medals and certificates.

I have been truly blessed in my life to have had parents that allowed me to follow my heart. They always encouraged me to pursue my dreams. They were supportive and gave me the courage to just be me. I left school at 16 and went onto college but they didn't try to stop me because they knew how passionate I was. Even one of my friends said things like "You could do better than be a hairdresser" or "You are quite clever; you could do more with your life." Hairdressing was known as something that people did if they weren't academic but what about doing something that ignites passion and excitement in our work?

Thankfully, I ignored my well-meaning friend and followed my heart. But this gives you an example of how labels and other people's opinions of those labels could affect our decisions and ultimately our whole lives.

Some years later a few of my old school friends and I met up, and it was lovely to hear what everyone was doing and what they had done with their lives. One particular friend said that she'd had a similar evening with friends the year before. They had talked about all the people in our high school year and were discussing who had become the most successful in life and seemingly they all agreed it was me. I was blown away. What me? I was just living my life with passion, following my dreams, I was not hungry for business success or any recognition, I was just following my heart.

When we follow our hearts instead of chasing a title or label to make us feel worthy, we are so much happier and we never have to call 'work' work. I can sit here for what feels like minutes and check the time and two hours have passed. This is my work yes, but it is not work to me. If I would not get paid (well I might not), it would never stop me.

So, chase passion and follow your heart and let the labels go. Don't choose your life's path for the title only, work will always be work until you make it your passion.

Health and wellness

Labels also hold us back when it comes to our health and well-being. They create barriers that block us from improving or growing due to a limited mindset. For example, I labelled myself as an asthmatic so I never even tried to run. Running for me is my greatest escape and my instant mood lifter, but because of the asthma label, I missed out on it for years due to my limiting beliefs.

Our ill health can also make some of us feel significant when we would otherwise feel invisible to those around us, and we hold on to it as if it is a comfort blanket. We think that having a label attached to us gives us a free pass to complain openly, and look for sympathy.

Just as a child misbehaves so they can get some attention, we can subconsciously hold on tight to our illness so we too can get some attention. Bad health can feel better than feeling non-existent and insignificant, but we are relinquishing control over our lives and health.

Also, for some reason people use their health conditions as excuses for not being their best. When they are diagnosed with certain conditions, they wear the label proudly like it's their "get out of jail free card", so they can stop trying to be healthy. For example, if a person has an underactive thyroid, they have to work a little harder to keep their weight stable but they still have full control over what they eat and drink and how much they exercise. But the trouble is that when they are diagnosed and have a name for why they are feeling bad or find it difficult to keep their weight down, they think they have no control. They stop trying altogether and blame their condition. If they removed the label however, or decide that they were not going to be labelled, they could gain back control of their bodies and health. I am not saying it is easy. I am saying that if we believe that we will gain weight due to our condition, we will gain weight. If we believe that it will not determine the quality of our life and health, then we will not let it.

Sometimes, instead of trying to overcome our health condition, we use it as an excuse for not being well. We take a pill and hope that it goes away but we are still responsible for our own bodies and our own health.

My niece Angelica has been living with Leukaemia for over ten years now and instead of allowing her illness to control her, she changed her life to control her illness. She studied nutrition of natural medicine and not only helped herself to be fit and well, she also spends her days helping others. She has taken her life and made the very best she can of it and has great faith. She has come to terms with the fact that she may not live life as long as she had hoped but fights every day and works hard at being her very best. When she was diagnosed, she could have complained and let the illness take control of her but she took it and used it to shape herself into this incredibly beautiful and strong being that spreads so much love and inspires everyone within her reach. She is an example of an incredible human being and living proof that we can fight back and conquer.

She talks about being grateful for her illness because it helped her to see the true value of life and wastes no time sweating the small stuff.

No matter what labels we wear, we can always conquer. We can question those labels and even re write them. We are not what we are labelled as. We are free. We are ever growing forces of strength that are in control of our lives, our health, and ultimately our destiny.

My Health and Well Being

1. On a scale of 1–10 how happy are you with your health and body? 1 being I am deeply disappointed with the way I look and feel, 10 being I feel amazing most days and I am happy with the way I look.

2. What level would you like to be on that scale and why?

3. How would you feel if you were at a level 1 and why would you not want to feel this way?

4. Close your eyes for a few minutes and imagine you are at a big event with all your friends and family. You are completely happy with your body and health and you are no longer comparing yourself to others. Describe how you look and feel as you walk into the room (in as much detail as possible).

a)   How do you feel about your body shape?

b)   What are you wearing?

c) Describe the look on your face and the way you are walking.

d) What emotions are you feeling?

5. Write down three reasons why you need a healthy body? For example: To provide me with energy to do what I want to do with my life; to prevent illness

a.
b.
c.

6. What are my energy levels like at the moment and how strong do I feel? For example: I have high energy levels and I feel like I am doing what is right for me, or I am tired a lot and struggle to get up in the morning.

7. What is my personal vision of 'my ideal body' for me and why?
    For example: My ideal body would be to look lean in a swimsuit on the beach because I'd be free to have fun without being aware of my size and shape.

8. What would I be able to do if I was my ideal body size that I feel I can't do presently? For example: I could wear X or I could run a marathon.

9. If I continue living my life, the way I do at the moment, how will I look and feel in:

Five years?

Ten years?

10. If I make changes now, how will it benefit me in the future?

11. If I am being totally honest with myself, what three small steps could I take to get me started so I can be happy with my body, health and energy levels to take me through the rest of my life?
For example: I could start to walk more; eat more vegetables or stop eating sugary processed foods.

a.
b.
c.

12. If I need help in getting my health and body on track, where can I go or who can I ask for help and support?

13. I deserve to treat myself and my body with the kindness it deserves because...

14. Imagine that you are in your forties or fifties and you are looking at yourself in the mirror and you are not happy with the way you look and feel. Now imagine you had the chance to go back in time for only five minutes to talk to yourself as you are now. What health advice would you give them?

Great Reasons to Adopt a Healthy Lifestyle

1. To look your very best now, and in the future.
2. To feel the best that you can feel, mind, body and spirit.
3. To have abundant energy and vitality for life.
4. To retain your youth as the years add on.
5. To feel attractive, confident and alive.
6. To have clear radiant skin.
7. To have mental clarity and direction in life.
8. To give your body the best protection against illness and disease.
9. To feel physically strong.
10. To live a full and happy life by choosing what you want to do, instead of what your body allows you to do.

Daily Habits

The difference between successful people and not so successful people has nothing to do with their upbringing, their DNA, or the opportunities that they are given, it is all down to their daily habits. Whether a person has a strong and fit physical body, an unshakable mindset, or a highly successful business, it's all down to what they focus on and what they consistently do every single day.

As I talked about before, the actor Chris Hemsworth (Thor) will most likely have a gruelling schedule to maintain his perfectly sculpted body. It is part of his job to maintain his physical form so whether he loves it or not, he will stick to his daily routine and habits that are paramount to his current success. He will not just work out a couple of times a week, that is for sure.

We all have daily habits. It is our human nature and it is what shapes us literally and figuratively. But we choose whether to create good habits to shape us into who we want to be, or let the bad habits control the outcome of our lives, our health and our destiny. Once we decide what we really want, it is just a matter of changing our habits to take us in the direction we want to go. But if our reasons are weak and we don't have a compelling enough reason to succeed, then we are likely to give up soon after we start. Often people don't realise how precious their lives are until they are threatened.

One of my friends used to love socialising and drank and smoked quite a lot but when he was 37 years old, he had a heart attack. He looked perfectly healthy and was not overweight so it was a shock for us all, not just him. He was told that if he didn't change his lifestyle, he would likely have another heart attack, so from one day to the next the drink and cigarettes were gone for good.

He didn't have to decide to change his habits, his body decided for him, but it nearly cost him his life.

For Chris Hemsworth, good health habits are a choice as they are essential, and his role as Thor is dependent on it. If he chooses to give up his role then he can also give up his workout routine and his healthy eating habits. I do not know anything about this man, but I do not need to know him to know that he has good daily habits, it is clearly evident. Not one person has ever come out of the womb with a lean, sculpted body. Success in all areas of life is created through consistently sticking to good habits.

If we want to change our lives in any way, we *have* to change our daily habits and rituals. When we begin each day in the right way for mind, body and spirit we can create better days, and a happier and healthier future. Our mind and body is like a fuel tank, so what we feed it with first thing every morning determines the quality of our days and our lives. We can fill our tank with fuel that will enhance our performance, or hinder it. We decide whether we want to run smoothly at a high-performance level or shuffle along getting through each day. Our performance is not only affected by what we eat, but also through what we fuel our minds and hearts with.

We say "we are what we eat", meaning that by filling our bodies with bad quality and unhealthy foods, we create bad quality and unhealthy bodies, true? Well, the same goes for our state of mind and heart. If we fill them with negative content from either social media or TV, like watching the news (with all the bad things going on in the world), then we are creating an unhealthy and negative mind.

When we wake up and fill our hearts and minds with things that cleanse and nourish us, we are fuelling them with positivity and goodness. It makes sense doesn't it.

We all have daily rituals whether they are good ones or bad but *we* choose what they are. If we want to improve our lives, to be happier and healthier, then changing our rituals to align with that outcome is the first step.

My Morning Rituals

We can each create daily rituals and habits that work for us but it is important that we prime ourselves for the day. Just as some painters use primer when painting walls to give the paint a good base before putting the paint on to improve the results, we need to prime our days to improve our results. When I spent my time in network marketing, I was introduced to a variety of trainings and books that I learned a lot from, and also how like-minded I am to a lot of successful people. I read the book 'The Miracle Morning'. This book included 18 interviews with highly successful people that were rated in the top 1% of network marketing leaders in America. What I learned was that every single one of them had set morning rituals that primed them for each day and optimised their work and performance. Some of the rituals and habits included:

- Prayer
- Meditation
- Healthy breakfast

- Exercise
- 30 minutes reading self-development books
- Listening to personal growth audios
- Affirmations
- Bible study
- Yoga
- Visualisation
- Journaling
- Gratitude

One thing that they all had in common was that they all wake up early. They wake up and take charge of the day and don't let the day be in charge of them. Success in any area of life begins with good habits so this is the best place to start. I cannot tell you what you should do, I can only tell you what I do to give you an idea.

- 6 am start or earlier
- Prayer… As soon as I wake up, I say a prayer of thanks. I thank God for this day, my life, my body and health and that of my family also. I pray for strength and guidance to being my best and giving my best to the world.
- I read a few pages of a personal growth book of some kind. (I also read before I go to sleep).
- I get up and have a glass of aloe vera, or a lemon water and prepare oats for myself and the kids.
- I go to my desk open my gratitude journal and spend time writing down three things that I am truly grateful for and write my world into existence (will explain later)
- I wake my children up and have breakfast with them and watch Darren Daily to kick start our day.
- Go for a 30-minute walk or run.

Primed.
So, what do I mean by "I write my world into existence"?

Some people say affirmations that help themselves to get into a good state, and say things like: "I am beautiful and successful; I am strong and powerful; I am a force of love and light in the world; I am becoming healthier every day!" and they say their personal affirmations out loud to themselves often throughout the day. I sometimes do this too when I need to be at my best but I like to write. I love the flow of pen to paper and I believe it connects the brain to the heart. I write down a reminder of who I am and who I am striving to become. It varies depending on what is in my heart and where I am on my journey but here is an example:

"Today is a wonderful day and truly magical things are going to happen. I am a happy and powerful being in control of my life, my health, my body, my mind, my actions, my reactions, my emotions, my happiness levels and my destiny. I live a life of love, balance and harmony as a mother, wife, writer, teacher and coach. My words and teachings enter into the hearts of people to help them to realise their personal power to improve their lives. My books will become international bestsellers so millions of people throughout the globe can have a simple guide to creating happy and healthy lives for themselves. Everything I need and want to achieve in life is within my power to create. I am grateful for…"

Writing in such a manner allows me to see all the good in my life and to remind me daily of my hand in my own destiny. Most of us know what we should do but a daily reminder to ourselves, from ourselves, is a good kick-start to the day.

Imagine if I had very different morning rituals. Let's say, for example, that every morning when my alarm goes off, I have a habit of pressing the snooze button and manage to sneak in another 20 minutes sleep. When I finally open my eyes, I pick up my phone to see what has been going on, on social media while I slept, to see if I have any new likes or comments. When I jump out of bed, 20 minutes later because I lost track of the time, I make myself a strong coffee to wake myself up while listening to the news on the TV. All the negativity is entering my mind and heart and I wonder what a horrible world we now live in.

I finish my coffee and rush to get ready for the day skipping breakfast as time has gotten away from me yet again.

How do you think my day would go if I had this as my morning ritual in comparison to beginning a day with a mind and body fuelled with the best quality ingredients?

Getting up a little earlier each day to take time for ourselves is essential to our well-being. Not only does it set us up for a happy, positive and productive day, it gives us time to think about and care for ourselves. Our bodies are the most valuable possession that we will ever own so making time to take care of our mind, body and soul is paramount.

So many people treat their pets and cars better than they treat their bodies yet they wonder why they feel lifeless and lack energy and enthusiasm. Would you expect your cars to run if they had no fuel? How efficiently would they run if you used poor quality fuel? Would you be surprised if they didn't do their job?

Would you feed your beloved pet fizzy, sugary drinks or chocolate? Would you consider not taking your dog for daily walks to get their exercise? If not, why not? It wouldn't kill them. Well not instantly. If you mistreated your pet you would risk not only their well-being but also risk having them taken away from you due to neglect. Does your pet deserve to be treated better than you? Do you value the life of your pet more than you value your own life?

Working on our bodies alone is not enough, we also have to learn to truly value ourselves and value our bodies, our minds and who we are as people. We are all precious beings and we need to be treated with the tender loving care that each of us deserve, especially by ourselves.

How well do I treat myself?

1. On a scale of 1–10, how well do I treat myself? (1 being I put no thought into my well-being at all, 10 being I do the best I can and have good daily habits to ensure my well-being)

2. How do I usually start my day?

3. How do I feel emotionally and physically at the moment due to my current morning habits? (For example, I leap out of bed with energy and excitement for life, or I wake up tired and wish I could sleep all day.)

4. How would I *like to feel* throughout the day, mind, body and spirit? (Examples, I would like to have more energy; think more positively; to feel happier)

    Body...
    Mind...
    Spirit...

5. What small changes can I make starting today and do every day, that will improve my life? For example:

    a. Mind... Read a self-development book, watch a motivational YouTube video while getting ready for the day.

a) Mind?
b) Body?
c) Spirit?

What Is Beauty?

True beauty is the essence of a kind and loving heart and soul that shines out through our eyes onto our faces and has nothing to do with the outside. It makes no difference how old we are, how much make-up we wear, how expensive our clothes are or how fit and toned our bodies are, if we have ugliness in our hearts and minds, we are ugly and most people can see it. True beauty can be seen through the soul, in our words and in our actions. Of course we have to take care of our bodies and make the best of ourselves but no matter how picture perfect we think we are on the outside, the ugly within us cannot be camouflaged. No amount of make-up or clever dressing can hide the monster within. If you want to be more attractive, work more on the inside and it will show on the outside.

We are often blinded by looks and we don't always look deeper to see the soul of a person, but when we are looking for someone to love and share our lives with, we need to look beyond appearance. If we are fortunate to live a long life our looks will fade, our hair will go grey, our bodies will age but when we are beautiful on the inside, nothing changes. In fact, we become more beautiful as we grow in wisdom and knowledge as we age.

Have you ever watched the film 'Beauty and the Beast'? When the Beast turns back into human did you feel a sense of loss? I know I certainly did and my daughter felt the same. Throughout the movie we had come to love 'The Beast' just as Bella had, and we were actually sad to see him transform into a human again.

As we go through life and make a slow and subtle transformation in our appearance, we have to remember that beauty comes from the heart and has nothing to do with what is on the surface.

You can however preserve your young skin, your young bodies and your young minds by taking care of them in the best way that you possibly can, to avoid unnecessary future pain and suffering. The way I see it is that if we give ourselves the best chance at being healthy and maintaining our youth, then we can live in peace knowing that we gave life our best shot, no matter how the future turns out. We will never regret taking care of ourselves, and if we don't, we cannot go back and change the past, so decide now how you want the course of your life to go. We deserve to be treated with love, by ourselves for ourselves. We are worth the effort and sacrifice.

Mask or Make-Up

As I look round at some young women today with the contoured make-up, fully applied eyebrows and false eyelashes, I wonder what goes on in their hearts and minds. I wonder why they feel the need for so much make-up. Why they feel the need to paint a mask on their faces to cover their true beauty.

- Is it because they want to hide who they are?
- Is it to be equal to everyone else?
- Is it to disguise themselves as someone else?
- Is it to give them confidence?
- Is it simply because they want to look on-trend? If so, why?

I find it fascinating and a little troubling to be completely honest as social media is bombarded with pouty selfies and booties that are the main event. I would love to sit down and talk to these girls and find out what is really going on in their hearts and minds. What are they in need of and what is missing in their lives? Love? Attention? Confirmation of their beauty? A label to make them feel good about themselves?

We all have a need to feel loved and to feel significant, to feel there is a point to our lives, and we go to great lengths to find these things, but all too often we are looking for the world to provide something that only we can give ourselves. Once we realise that we have to: First know who we are, second love who we are, and third be who we are, we are then able to live our lives freely and no longer look for the world to label us as worthy, because deep down we know we are worthy.

I also wonder at what point in a relationship do these young women start to reveal what they really look like, essentially removing their mask. When do they start to reveal the real person underneath? It must also be very confusing for the people they date. It must feel a bit scary for them as they are not quite sure what is underneath all the make-up. Have you ever seen those videos on social media of incredibly talented make-up artists that manage to paint a young woman's face on an old lady? It really freaks me out but it gives me hope for the future as I get older. LOL.

I know we are not what we look like, but why hide? The way I see it is that if people love us for being our natural selves, anything that we do to enhance our beauty is good, but if people are attracted to the made-up version of us, how will we ever know if they like us for being our natural selves?

The word 'make up' itself means that it is fantasy. When we make up a story we tell untruths, correct? Well what does that say about make up on our faces? I am all for make up to enhance and define our features. It can be beautiful and feminine, but when a whole other face has been painted on top of ours it makes us wonder what, or who we are hiding from.

We may also use our clothes as a way to stand out, be noticed and feel significant but we also have to ask ourselves if we are dressing this way to feel good about ourselves or to gain attention. What kind of attention are we looking for? What kind of message are we hoping to send to the people that see us? Clothes are a way to express who we are without words and to frame our personalities, so decide what kind of person you are and frame yourself in that way. I remember meeting up with my beautiful niece when she was about 14 and she had a really low-cut top on so I pointed at her boobies and said, "If we were meant to see them Sweetheart, they'd be on your face!" I made her laugh *and* she got the point.

I am not here to judge in any way, I would just love it if every single one of us loved ourselves for who we really are regardless of how we look. To give us the best chance of living a full, happy and healthy life. But in order for us to do this we have to come face to face with our fears and insecurities, overcome them and love ourselves wholeheartedly.

Dare to Be You

Being ourselves can be scary as we are opening ourselves up to rejection if people do not like the flawed and imperfect beings that we are. But what would you rather have, an arena of people that love the character you are playing or a roomful of people that love you for who you truly are? Do you think having an arena full of people cheering and screaming would make you feel more loved than being cuddled up on a sofa with the people that love you no matter how terrible you look?

I spent a lot of my life hiding myself from the world in fear of not being good enough, clever enough or beautiful enough, but I was burying my true self and I was terribly unhappy. Once I let go of my fears and started to love myself and just be myself, all the blocks that were imprisoning me just melted away and I felt so much freedom and love. I no longer feared not being liked and no longer looked for a thumbs up from the world because I am happy with who I am and what I do. Would I be writing this book if I feared being judged? Some of you will love this book and some may (well doubtful) hate it, but only by being myself am I free to even write it.

So be brave. Be the best version of you and shine from within. Believe me when I say that this is the ultimate place to be… to be free from fear of judgement from others, and be free to be yourself and feel truly alive. When you love yourself for the person that is deep within your soul, warmth will surround you like a blanket of love.

INTIMACY

To me, having an intimate relationship with another human being is not so much a physical act but a spiritual one. It's when two committed souls come together in an expression of love. A sacred act between two souls that love each other completely.

I am not going to discuss the physical aspects of an intimate relationship but I want to touch on the emotions attached to it. Sex is sex, and love is love and we must not confuse the two. This is where a lot of people get confused and mistake sex for love. Some also feel pressured to have an intimate relationship because that's 'just what you do' but we have to listen to our hearts and not to our bodies in this case. This is *not* one of those times that we should "feel the fear and do it anyway". If we feel the fear, our heart is telling us that it is not in alignment with our true self.

I am not telling you if and when you should have intimate relations with people but to make sure that your decisions are in alignment with your guiding principles to build your self-worth (not your ego), and that you are doing it for the right reasons. Not because you feel under pressure to, or in order to feel loved and desired. Just like I said before, we are 'The One' so 'putting out' will not lead to being filled with love and attention, it will ultimately make us feel more unloved and of less worth. It would be like eating sweets instead of a meal in the hope of feeling nourished and satisfied. It may help for a little while but we are still left unnourished, unsatisfied and empty inside. Just as disease grows when we feed it sugar, our lack of self-worth grows by feeding it anything other than the love that we truly deserve from ourselves and another human being.

The advantage of living a hundred or so years ago is that marriage generally came before sex so both parties knew that they were loved completely and that they were valued but now things are very different. It was black and white then but now it's 50 shades of grey. No matter what the world is doing, what your friends are doing, what the movies are doing, *you* are in control of your life and your body and so you must choose what is right for you.

There is also a misconception that males just want sex and females want love but whatever gender a person is, we all want to feel loved and to feel that deep con- nection. People that do sleep around are not necessarily bad people but perhaps need to prove something to themselves, are desperately seeking to feel significant in some way, or are trying to fill that emptiness inside of them (no pun intended), but living this way creates more emptiness. They too are seeking 'The One' within.

I know as a woman that we think we can fill a man's heart by loving him enough but if he doesn't love who he is in his heart and know his worth as a human being, he will always feel empty, and we can never fill that emptiness for him. I cannot speak from a male perspective but my male friends are just as vulnerable as women but perhaps fear being seen as less masculine if they reveal their insecurities. Again, if each of us tear off the labels we have and just be ourselves no matter who we are, what age we are, what gender we are, we will feel so much freer which will enable us to live life with joy and feel fully alive.

Your Commitment and Promise

Just as you made promises earlier in the book to honour yourself through your worth, and to honour your heart, now it is time to honour your body through making a promise to yourself... We only have one shot at life and this is the vessel that our Creator has given us. It is our one and only chance to treat it as it deserves to be treated. No matter how flawed it is or how badly we have mistreated it in the past, from today on we can decide to honour it.

My personal promise...

I promise to honour my body and to continue to take care of my health and well-being as I have done in the past. I will only eat good quality healthy foods that will provide my body with what it needs to be strong, healthy, durable and provide me with abundant energy and vitality. I promise to keep moving daily to keep me running smoothly with ease. I promise to use only natural ingredients on my skin and hair, to avoid using chemicals that create toxins within my system and can compromise my health. I will treat my body with respect and will not allow others to mistreat it in any way. I will always remember it is a priceless gift. I promise to do all within my power to nourish my body with all that it needs to stay youthful and beautiful.

Now it's your turn...

A PROMISE TO HONOUR MY BODY.

I promise...

Signature...
Date...

TASTY TREAT RECIPES

Chocolate Milkshake

Ingredients

1 large ripe banana.
250 ml of unsweetened vegetable milk (almond, soya, rice milk, etc.).
1 tablespoon of unsweetened cacao powder.
A few ice cubes (optional).

Method

Throw into the blender and whiz up until smooth.

Tips:

1   I always keep some frozen banana slices in the freezer and throw a few in when I want a refreshingly cold smoothie, but don't drink really cold drinks in the winter as it can create cold and damp inside which can cause bloating, block digestion and weaken your body and functions.

2   Carob is a great substitute for chocolate with all of the chocolaty taste with none of the stimulants. Replace the tablespoon of cacao powder with a tablespoon of carob powder.

Chocolate and Hazelnut Pudding

Ingredients

4 cups of soya milk.
2 eggs.
1 tablespoon of solid honey.
60g corn flour.
20g unsweetened cacao powder.
A few roasted hazelnuts (crushed).

Method

- Heat the milk in a pan but do not boil.
- Whisk up the two eggs in a large bowl and then add the honey, corn flour and cacao and continue to whisk until smooth.
- Once smooth, add the warm milk to the bowl and mix before returning the whole mixture to the pan.
- Bring the mixture to the boil and turn the heat back down to minimum continually stirring until it thickens (1 minute or so) and then remove from the heat.
- Pour the delicious chocolaty cream into glasses or bowls and sprinkle over the chopped hazelnuts.
- Leave to set, and store in the fridge.

Panna Cotta

Ingredients

Four cups of soya milk (or another milk of your choice). I find half goat's milk and half soya milk makes the best combination
60 grams corn flour
80 grams of honey or agave
Half a vanilla pod (seeds) or the equivalent
200g Strawberries

Squeeze of lemon juice
Agave or honey to taste

Method

- Warm the milk in a pan leaving a little behind to dissolve the corn flour
- In a bowl put the corn flour, cold milk, vanilla and agave syrup and whisk until smooth.
- Add the warm (not boiled) milk to the bowl and transfer back to the pot and bring to the boil…stir until it thickens
- Allow to cool for five minutes before pouring into moulds or glasses
- Leave to cool and then leave in the fridge to set

For the sauce:

- Chop up strawberries and whiz up in the blender with a squeeze of lemon juice and a tablespoon of agave syrup.
- Bring to the boil and then take off the heat and allow to cool.
- To serve turn out the set Panna Cotta onto a plate and spoon over the cold strawberry sauce. (Or serve in a glass with the sauce on the top.)

Chocolate Balls

Ingredients

250g raisins
100g oats
2 heaped tablespoons of unsweetened cacao powder
50g grated coconut
50g almonds or other nuts.
Extra grated coconut for coating the balls

Method

- Throw the raisins in a food processor and whizz until the raisins are broken up.
- Add the remaining ingredients and blend until a dough has formed.
- Using damp hands, roll into bite size balls and then roll in more coconut and leave to firm in the fridge for 24 hours.

They can be stored in the fridge for up to two weeks.

Alternatives:

Add two to three drops of edible essential peppermint oil, or orange oil, to vary the flavours to mint-choc or orange-choc.

Love Lesson #6
My Dream Life

"True success is living life doing what you love."

Living a dream life has been the focus of my entire life since I was a little girl. I didn't know what I was here for or if I was even meant to be here but I was always determined to fight for happiness. Thankfully I haven't really changed that much. I still have big dreams and big goals that evolve and grow as I do. I absolutely refuse to live a mediocre life of just getting by. I have fallen from time to time but I don't stay down for long. I pick myself up, brush myself off and keep going. Health is my number one priority because without good health I cannot be free to live life the way I choose, but to me living a dream life is the absolute pinnacle of success, regardless of how much money I earn or the level of my worldly success. Because each and every one of us have a different idea of what success looks like, each of our dream lives can look very different too.

I was living my dream life for years as a stay-at-home mummy with my beautiful little children, cooking them healthy meals, keeping my home and growing my own organic vegetables, going for walks and playing with them day in and day out. I was with them for their first words, their first steps, taught them to do their first every-thing and I was in my element. It hadn't always been part of my plan to be a full-time mummy. When I was a teenager, I didn't want to get married or have children as I was focused on becoming a great success in life and having a great career, but as I grew up, I started to change my mind. The moment I made the decision was the day my nephew was born. I walked into the hospital and saw this beautiful little human being and fell in love instantly. That day I knew that motherhood was for me.

Being a mother to young children was hard work but I knew exactly what I wanted motherhood to be like for me and I achieved it. I had very little money but living my life as a mother to my babies was far more valuable to me than having money to buy things that I did not need.

No matter what we desire, no one else can tell us what our dream lives look like, or if they are achievable or not. I remember being asked what I was doing with my life and when I proudly said I was a full-time mummy, a look of horror spread across this woman's face. She asked if I was having trouble finding work but I explained that I made this choice, that being a full-time mummy was my dream but she didn't understand me at all. She didn't need to understand, I needed to know what was in my heart and live my life my way, regardless of other people's opinions. Only *we* know the desires of our heart, and only *we* can create our version of our dream lives.

I was truly happy for many years but as my children grew, I began to lose my sense of purpose. They no longer wanted me to be with them 24/7. I was no longer the centre of their world. They no longer needed me full time so I began to question my purpose again. Who am I other than a mother? What do I have to offer the world? What are my gifts and talents that could be of value? Because I had become so engrossed in motherhood, I had forgotten to take care of me and began to lose my self-confidence so every time I searched for answers to my questions, I came up blank. I felt lost and scared because I was focused on what I didn't have and what I couldn't do, so I crumbled.

This was a new emotion for me because I had spent most of my life determined to succeed, which I had, but this time I couldn't see the bigger picture. Because I failed to keep reviewing my vision of my dream life and to keep growing and learning, I got stuck. I had naively thought that when I was living my dream life, I could stop trying. I thought that I could just stay still but the reality is that when we stop moving forward, we fall. Just like when we ride a bike, we have to keep moving forward in order to maintain balance. If we stop pedalling, we fall. Because I fell, I had to pick myself up off the ground, rediscover who I was again and create a new vision, a new dream and a new and improved version of me, and that's what I did. But as I lay on the metaphorical ground and looked around, I realised I was not alone. In fact, I was surrounded by so many people that lay helpless on the ground beside me. Some due to falling, and some had never even got on their bike in the first place because of unfounded fear.

Once I had worked on knowing who I was again, and loving who I am, I was able to see that I had not lost my power, I had just stopped playing the game of life. I then took the control panel back into my own hands and I was back in charge. If I wanted to live my dream life and be happy, I had to take responsibility. No one was going to hand me happiness on a plate, I had to earn it.

Working on myself and working on my dream made me realise that I could help others to do the same. I could reach out to those that were on the ground next to me when I had fallen. Because I had worked obsessively on refuelling my mind and spirit using all my past knowledge and experience and by immersing myself into studying the path to happiness, I knew 100% that I could help to lift others too by teaching them how.

So, what I thought was one of the darkest moments of my life when I was lost, turned out to be a blessing in disguise, just as my near-death experience had been almost 20 years earlier. If I had not experienced that level of darkness and lack of self-love, I would never have discovered my gift or found my calling.

I like to believe that God isn't punishing us when things don't go our way; He just gives us a hard nudge from time to time so we can wake up and take stock of our lives and rethink our direction. Life doesn't happen 'to us', it happens 'for us'. All things good and bad, happen for a reason and the more we look for ways to grow from our experiences, the better our lives can become.

All that I went through and all that I have learned in my time on the earth so far has led me to where I am today. To becoming a certified life coach, teacher and writer, and led me to creating and writing this very book.

So far we have learned about: Knowing who you are; knowing your true worth; understanding the power of your heart and emotions; and taking care of your body which will lead you to living your dream life, but now we have to bring all these together to reveal why *you* are here. What you desire from life, how you want to live and to knowing your higher purpose.

You have a choice whether to skim through this book, throw it to one side or leave it on the bookshelf gathering dust. Or you can immerse yourself in its pages, drink in the knowledge and teachings, highlighting the parts that mean the most to you, and use it as a life treasure map. We all have free will and none of us are forced to live amazing lives but if you live by this book, use it as it is designed to be used, and continue to learn and grow, *you* too can create a life of abundance.

We are each here for a good reason but it's up to us whether we take the time to discover *who* we are and *why* we are here, to either create an abundant life or to endure a life of 'just getting by'.

Living a dream life for me is living life on my terms, being free to be me, to do what I choose to do with all that I have. To spend my life feeling the best that I can feel, doing what I love, with who I love.

I write, I teach and I speak because I have abounding passion to help people to realise their power to create a life being abundantly happy. I am the happiest person I know but not because I have everything that I always wanted, but because I am being my true self, and living my life with purpose. I know I am making a difference to the lives of others through my work and sharing my love. Even if my work touches only one heart and transforms only one life, I know that I have made a difference. I know I am living my purpose.

My Purpose

Some of us know exactly who we are and why we are here, and some of us struggle to know either, but when we love ourselves and others fully, giving all that we can, we can live purposeful lives. We also need to work on ourselves becoming better every day. God made us exactly how we were meant to be in life in order for us to play the part that we are meant to play in the world. That does not mean we should not grow and improve, that is our choice, but it's essential that we remember that God does not make mistakes. Whether you believe in a higher power or not, we all have a purpose and reason for being. It may take some of us longer to know what our reason for being is, and some may never really know why, but we have to trust that we play a major part in life somehow.

Tom's Story
Tom was a man who had everything that he needed to make him happy. A wonderful and caring wife, two beautiful children, a good job and a good income but he felt empty and lost within himself, and was not happy. He needed more somehow. He needed to feel complete, whole even, but instead of looking within himself to find it, he made some bad life choices which led him down the wrong road.

Consequently, his wife left him and moved away taking the kids with her. He had made some mistakes and now had to live with the repercussions of his actions. He began drinking heavily every day to dull the pain and his life spiralled out of control and even further downwards.

Within a matter of months, he'd lost his wife, his kids, his friends and finally his job. He was left broken, angry and alone. Because his behaviour had been so appalling, everyone he cared about wanted nothing more to do with him. He hated himself so much that one dark day while he was sitting alone in the park, he made the decision to end his life. He hated his life, he hated people but most of all he hated himself.

Why live? he thought, I have nothing to live for so what's the point...? The world will be better off without me!

As he stood up to go home to end his life, he reached into his pocket and took all the money that he had on him and handed it to a poor homeless woman lying on a nearby bench, after all he didn't need money where he was going. The homeless woman looked up at him, looked at the handful of money and began to cry and as he walked away, she shouted:

"Thank you! Thank you! You are an angel and I am so grateful for your kindness. You have no idea how much this means to me!"

Tom looked back, half smiled and waved, but at that moment, for the first time in months, he felt a spark of light inside of him. The beginnings of a genuine smile began to appear on his face, and something within him awakened.

As he walked away, he noticed a lightness in his step instead of the usual heavy feeling of dragging his body around. He realised that HE can make a difference to someone. Maybe only a drop in the ocean, but it was a drop. That one small act of kindness and those few words of thanks was enough to stop Tom from taking his own life that day. His heart was reignited with love and a new journey began in a quest to find inner peace and happiness in his life through serving and loving others. In the depths of his darkness, that tiny spark of light gave him not only a will to live, but the will to transform himself to become the man that he knew he could be.

Every day for weeks after, Tom went back to the park and to that very bench in search of the lady to thank her for saving his life but he never saw her again. He secretly hoped that those few pounds that he handed her on that dark night many months earlier had somehow saved her life too...but he would never know.

Now, imagine how that homeless woman would have felt if she had known that she had saved a man's life that day? Just as Tom did not know how much of a difference those few pound notes made to this woman; she had no idea that her kind words of thanks were enough to give a man significance in a world where he felt like he was worth nothing.

So, every kind word spoken and every kind act that we perform can have an enormous impact on the lives of others as well as our own. We are all meant to be and we are all of great worth even if we cannot always see the evidence of it. Each and every one of us play an important role in life, and even if we don't know how or why, we have to trust that we make a difference.

At times when I was really young, I used to wonder why I existed. I used to feel like I never really belonged anywhere. I was different from my sisters, and even though I had lots of friends, I was different to them too and I never felt of any worth. We were a mixed-race family with darker skin than others and I always felt like a foreigner wherever I went. My sisters and I were subjected to bullying so I did my best just to stay under the radar. Even though I had lots of wonderful people around me I always felt 'different'. I wanted to fit in and be like everyone else, to blend in but it never happened. My friend once said to me with a big smile on her face:

"You've lived in Scotland for ages, it's like you are Scottish now. Not Chinese, Italian, or English (I was born in England and lived there until I was seven). You are Scottish like me!"

When she said that I was shocked. Her intentions were completely pure and she wanted me to feel good about myself but it made me wonder who I was. As a nine-year-old, these were the questions that I asked myself, to which I had no answers…

"Am I ashamed of my mum and dad? Am I ashamed of my roots and my foreign blood? Are 'normal' people better than me? What if I *am* different? Do I really want to be normal?"

The problem I had at that age was that I was like a square trying to fit into a round hole instead of accepting that I was a square.

Eventually I accepted that I was a square, and was happy being a square, and life began to make more sense. I started to see how blessed I was that I had such a wonderful rare heritage that allowed me to experience different cultures, incredible foods and countries.

At multiple times in my life, as I have grown and evolved, I have had to go back and re-evaluate what shape I am and what I discovered is that I am me, a shape with no name and no label, just as we all are. I am Nadia Wong, the one and only. Some may share my name, my blood, my ideas, even my life, but there is only one unique me.

We are all different shapes, sizes and colours. We are all beautiful and full of worth. There is a place and space in life for every single one of us as we are all of equal worth in the eyes of God, and we all have a purpose. Our self-doubt doesn't manifest because we are worthless, but because we are trying to live a life that we don't fit into. We are essentially trying to squeeze into, or feel lost in, a pair of jeans that are the completely wrong size and shape for us. If we cannot fit into ready-made clothes, we have to learn how to make our own clothes and make them to fit us instead of trying to be a regular fit. So, if we don't fit into an off the shelf life, we need to learn how to create our own life to fit around us, and this is what I did.

Whether we live our purpose through our job or in our free time, our value is the same but if we have to spend a third of our 24 hours a day working, we may as well spend it doing something we love, something that lights up our souls, something that makes us feel truly alive through sharing our gifts with others. I would rather spend my days doing something I love and get paid less than spend eight or more hours a day in a job I hate. We can always find ways to earn back our money but we can never earn back our time. Imagine a world where everyone did the job they loved. People would be happier, more cheerful, more helpful, more creative and so on, and the world would be a happier place to live.

I love what I do, and I would still do it if I did not get paid. In fact, writing this book takes faith in myself because essentially, I am working with the intention that it will be a success with no evidence that it will make money, but that does not stop me. My intentions are pure as I know that I have created a useful tool to navigate the young people of today through the maze of life. Nothing in life is a sure thing except death and taxes so any step we take in life, is taking a chance on us. When we know our intentions for life, believe in ourselves and our work and utilise our gifts and talents, there is no end to our potential success. When we love what we do we will never have to work a day in our lives. We can spend our days doing what we love and earn a living doing it.

My four steps to creating a dream life are:

DREAM
BELIEVE
ACT
RECEIVE

DREAM

Dreaming big and creating a clear vision of our dream life in our minds is how we begin to create great success in life. Imagine playing a video game without knowing the objective. Is it only to reach the end and not be killed? Is it to not only survive, but to gain points and win? Is it to collect items and build something of worth? Is it to save all the people, protect them, and become the hero? Until we actually know the point of the game, we will waste valuable time trying to figure it out and most likely give up as it would become boring and pointless. Once we know what we have to do, and why, then we can get on with it and not only enjoy the game, but have a thrilling time doing it. Well, life is the same. If we don't have a goal or objective, then what are our chances of winning at the game of life?

We all have big dreams when we are small whether we want to be a pop star, policeman, ballet dancer, movie star or a unicorn but as we grow and realise that we may not have what it takes, we give up and settle for a good sensible career just in case. We lay our dreams to one side and start to listen to the world instead of our hearts. Obviously, we change with time when we realise that being a unicorn is not an option but as for the other dreams we have, if we can dream it, we can achieve it. An amazing life won't just land in our laps, we have to go and create it. We have the power, we hold the keys, we are playing the game of life but we can only win if we play to win. We are the producer, director and writer in the movie of our own life and we can either choose to play the leading role as the hero or an extra that blends into the crowd in the background. At this age and stage in your life you have a whole life ahead of you to write yourselves an epic movie but first you need to know what the ending will be. There will be twists and turns, excitement and romance, wins and losses but *you* are writing the story and *you* choose the ending. It is vitally important that we write down clear goals for what we want in all areas such as work, home, lifestyle, health, money, to review them often and keep the destination clear in our minds always. We can change our goals as we go through life but we always need a clear destination in order for us to arrive where we want to be.

Essentially this book is you writing your story because up to this point you have written about who you are and who you want to become but now is the time to plan the ending. Is it a happy one or does it end in tears? *You* decide if it's a happily ever after.

BELIEVE

With faith, all things are possible. We can only achieve our dreams if we truly believe in them. A dream is only ever a dream if we don't live them out. All of our decisions in life are based on what we believe. We need faith in everything or we would never do anything.

- When we make a cake, we have faith it will rise nicely and taste delicious when it's finished.
- When we close our eyes at night, we have faith that we will wake up in the morning refreshed and energised.
- When we eat, we have faith that the food will nourish our bodies and fuel us for the day.
- When we get married, we have faith that our marriage will last and we will be part of a loving relationship for the rest of our lives.
- When we start a new journey, we have faith that we will get where we want to be, otherwise we would never take a single step forward.
- When we exercise, we have faith that it is doing our bodies good by making them stronger and healthier.
- When we jump in the car, we have faith that it will take us to our destination safely.
- When we read a self-awareness book, we have faith that our lives will improve in some way.

We would never do anything if we thought we would not get what we want, so in order to achieve, we must first have a clear picture in our minds of what we want to achieve, believe we deserve it and know with surety that it will come.

ACT

Once we have our crystal-clear vision and a strong belief system in our minds it is time to act. Success doesn't just happen by chance we have to make it happen. If we are overweight and struggle with health issues, it doesn't matter how much we want to be healthy, it won't just happen by itself. We have to decide what we want to achieve, make a plan, ACT, and consistently work on improving every day. Dreams will continue to stay dreams until we act on them to make them a reality.

I had the pleasure of reading an amazing book called 'The Top Five Regrets of the Dying' by Bronnie Ware in which she recounts stories of her work as a carer for terminally ill people by making their last weeks upon the earth as comfortable as possible. One of the biggest regrets expressed by those that were dying, regardless of their age, was, "I wish I'd had the courage to live a life true to myself, not the life others expected me to live."

I was not surprised by this statement because of my own personal experience, and I live my life by this principle. Since my brush with death, when I face difficult decisions in life, I imagine myself on my deathbed and I ask myself, "Will I regret I did this or be glad I tried?" I knew I would never regret doing good things so my choices were made easy. I make all major decisions with this in mind and it has served me well.

I gave up hairdressing 20 years ago because I stopped loving it. I wanted to live my dream life in the sunshine and move overseas, and also wanted to make my health my number one priority so I could prepare my body for having a family, but people thought I was crazy for walking away from a successful business. Countless people tried to talk me out of it but I never listened, and I am so glad I didn't.

"Why give up a highly successful and profitable business?" they would say, but to me financial success without fulfilment is failure. Why spend my days doing something I don't like anymore? Life is too short to live it unhappily. I had so much more I wanted to do with my life but if I didn't break free from my business I would never have moved forward.

I had dreams of being a full-time mother, being a motivational speaker, of writing books. I never knew how or when I would do these things but I did know I had to break free from hairdressing. I had to take a risk. My dreams could have stayed dreams and I could still be spending my days in my hair studio but when my heart left the job, I had to leave too and it was the best move I ever made. It was risky, I was taking a chance but I would rather spend my life chasing and working on my dreams and fail, than live a life of regrets. If I only dreamt of becoming an author and helping millions of people without starting to write a book, how would I ever know if my work could help others? It's a bit like having an invention in our heads and doing nothing about it...our ideas are of no worth if we do nothing with them, and we are helping no one. We may think we are clever for coming up with all these great ideas to change the world for the better in some way, but perhaps not so clever if we never use the ideas. A dream and goal is worth nothing without taking action. I love the following wise words from the wonderful Les Brown:

"The graveyard is the richest place on earth, because it is here you will find all the hopes and dreams that were never fulfilled, the books that were never written, the songs that were never sung, the inventions that were never shared, the cures that were never discovered, all because someone was too afraid to take that first step, keep with the problem, or determined to carry out their dream."

Giving in to fear of failing or listening to the opinions of others, is a sure way to kill our dreams. We have all that we need to succeed in our lives and we can all live our dream lives but we cannot leave it to chance. But where do we start? With a vision and clear picture of our dream life etched into our heart mind and soul, self-belief, and a plan.

RECEIVE

This is the part that we begin to reap what we have sown but in order to reap we have to be open and worthy to receive it. Knowing that we deserve success due to our hard work will open the channels to receiving it. To know we are good enough. To know with a surety of heart that this is our time to shine. If we go through life with a vague and ever-changing ending to our story, whether we get the girl/boy or not, whether we become wealthy or not, whether we get our dream life or not, then we will end up with a vague and ever-changing result. When we know exactly what we want and expect to hit the target, we will hit the target or get as close as possible to it. If we are not ready to receive it however and keep changing the target due to accepting less or making do, we will most likely be aiming our efforts in the wrong direction and miss altogether.

When we know success is coming, we will recognise it when it appears. We will know when the man or woman of our dreams appears, we will apply for that dream job, we will embrace new and exciting opportunities because we have our arms out ready to receive the blessings that we know we deserve, instead of walking past the love of our lives, not applying for that job or turning down an exciting opportunity. We have to be ready to receive these blessings.

Fear of success is very real and can often hold us back as we fear a different life, more pressure to be at our best and pressure to succeed. We may also fear setting ourselves up for disappointment or separating ourselves from our peers by stepping up to climbing the success ladder. Envy and jealousy from those around us can rear its ugly head when we succeed, so to avoid it, we stay back in the shadows afraid to step into the light. But jealousy and envy have nothing to do with who we are, it's the insecurities of those that envy us coming to life. But we cannot live in the shadows of our own soul to please others. The more we succeed in our own lives, the more we can give and share of ourselves.

After all, we can't share what we don't have.

If we are not ready to receive what we believe is rightfully ours, we could be distracted by looking further ahead and miss what is right in front of us. As we begin to reap the fruits of our labour, we also have to remember who we are, be true to ourselves and remember to stay humble. To never look down on another human being unless we are helping them up. To remember that we are no better or worse than any human being no matter who we are or what we achieve. We are not competing with others, we are challenging ourselves and being the best *we* can be, giving the best of ourselves to others. To remember that we all play a valuable part in life and to be grateful for all that we have and all that we are.

When we pray before a meal we say, "Thank you for the food that we are about to receive," which is a blessing of the food we know we will eat. So, saying "Thank you for the life that we are about to receive" is the blessing of a life that we know we will live with joy.

Gifts and Talents

Understanding what our gifts and talents are is the way to understand our purpose and create our vision. We are all unique and we all have gifts that can make this world better somehow but it's our choice whether to use them and develop them or to toss them aside as if they are of no value.

In the Bible, Jesus tells a story about a merchant that goes on a long trip, and while he is away, he trusts his three servants with his talents (gold coins), and asked them to take care of them.

He gives one servant five talents, the second servant two talents, and the third 1 talent according to their abilities.

The first servant worked hard and doubled his talents and now had ten.

The second also worked hard and doubled his talents and now had four.

The third, however, was afraid to lose the talent so he buried it to keep it safe and did nothing with it.

When the man returned, he called his servants and asked them what they had done with their talents.

When the first servant brought him ten talents the man was happy and rewarded him by making him a leader over many things and told him to go and live a happy life. When the second servant brought four talents the man again was happy and made him a leader over many things too, and told him to live happily also.

When the third servant presented him with his 1 talent however, the man was not happy. He was in fact extremely disappointed because this servant had buried his talent and did nothing with it. The man then took back the talent and gave it to the

149

first servant and sent the third servant away empty-handed.

We have all been blessed with unique gifts and talents in this life, but it's what we do with them that makes them valuable and makes us happy. If we go through life scared to use them, then we are wasting them. Instead, we have to work hard to develop them and use them to create something worthwhile, not bury them and hide them away from the world.

Let's say you have the most incredible gift and passion for singing but you never sing because you are fearful of what others say, or scared that you'll be criticised or ridiculed. You would not only be robbing yourself of the sense of achievement and the personal rewards, but you'd also be robbing the world of hearing your voice that could touch the hearts of many and put smiles on their faces.

Imagine you were given a gift of a helicopter which was sitting on the helipad on the roof of your house. You know it is there but until you learn to fly it, it is a complete waste. If you take the time to learn to fly, and land it correctly, imagine the kind of experiences you could have. You could fly high and see the world from a whole other perspective but only if you learn how to use it. Your talent, your passion, your gifts are your helicopter but unless you learn how to use them and develop them, they are left unused and your view of the world will be limited.

Let me give you an example of a more subtle gift or talent. I have always had the ability to see greatness and potential in people. I can somehow see into the hearts of good people and feel their souls. I can't really explain it but I know what I feel. I am able to bring the best out in others and help them to see this greatness for themselves. In my teens and twenties, I worked as a hairstylist but the part I loved most about my work, apart from the relationships I had with my clients, was developing young people. I loved the training part of hairdressing and helping my trainees to become masters of their work. I always knew I would teach one day but I didn't know what I would teach. But here I am teaching self-love, self-awareness, self-worth and teaching others how to work on developing themselves. Years later when I temporarily lost my way and I got caught in the fog of my own self-doubt, I could have given up and settled. After all I lived in Italy with wonderful food, amazing summer weather and the beach only 15 minutes away, but I felt unfulfilled inside. There was an emptiness in my soul and I needed to fill myself with love through living my true purpose. Imagine if I had been too scared to open myself up to the world and had buried my head (talent) in the sand, I wouldn't be doing what I am doing now and I certainly would not be sitting here writing this book. Nobody would have benefited from my work and I would have wasted all that I had been gifted with. Even if I make a difference to only one person in my lifetime, then my work will have been worthwhile.

Imagine all the amazing talented people out in the world that are not successful. They have dreams in their hearts but keep them locked away but why? Is it due to self-doubt? Fear of failure? Fear of rejection? Lack of motivation? Lack of opportunity? Think they are not smart enough? Not worthy enough? Not intelligent enough? Whatever their reason, they will feel some emptiness in their souls, like I did, if they don't follow the path that was destined for them. When we have a special gift, we naturally have a desire to share it with others but if we allow fear to stop us, then we are not free to be who we are. Our true selves feel trapped and frustrated and we feel imprisoned by our own fears. Nobody can remedy this but us. We have the key and we can unlock our potential at any time by revealing and developing our innermost gifts and talents. We as human beings are at our happiest not when we achieve our dreams, but when we pursue them. In our pursuit we grow and develop our authentic selves putting our power to the test. This is where excitement and the joy of expectation lies. It's that feeling of falling in love, not knowing but still moving forward in hopeful pursuit of what we love. Personally, I would rather live following my heart and fail, than never to try at all. To me never trying is the only true and ultimate failure.

When we witness other's success on a higher level, we may think to ourselves that they are lucky, but we have no idea how hard they have worked to get them to where they are. We are not only unique in our talents but also in our inner desires. Every highly successful person that has ever lived put hours and hours of work into perfecting their talent. Whether it be by playing a sport or a musical instrument, writing, speaking, sewing or dancing, time, consistent practise and dedication were put into developing their gifts and talents. I can guarantee that they also stepped out of their comfort zones time and time again, faced their fears, made some personal sacrifices and dealt with rejection before they made it. Making the most of our gifts and talents does take courage and hard work, and we will fall from time to time but picking ourselves up and pushing forward consistently, will take us a step closer to success.

Creating a Vision of My Dream Life

Imagine that you are planning a holiday of a lifetime. Think about all the questions that you would ask yourself before making any decisions. After all you wouldn't want to waste your time and money on a holiday you wouldn't enjoy. Would you?

What time of year would I go? Beach, skiing, hiking, biking, camping? Who do I want to go with? What countries do I want to visit? How much money do I want to spend? What kind of accommodation do I want? All inclusive? Bed and breakfast only? Do I want a pool or beach access? Quiet and relaxing or fun and lively? How long for? What kind of weather would I like? What kind of foods do I want to experience?

These are only just some of the questions that we ask before we plan a holiday, to enjoy our free time in the best way that we possibly can, but how much time do we spend asking ourselves questions about our dream lives so we can enjoy our lives the best way we can?

Imagine only having one holiday a year and not making any plans for it. What would we spend the entire time doing? Sleeping? Watching TV? Scrolling through social media posts? Before we know it, our time would be up and we would feel cheated out of a good holiday and most likely wish we'd been more organised or saved enough money to actually do something worthwhile with our time.

Well the same goes for our lives. If we don't take the time beforehand to plan our lives, what would we spend our lives doing? Working at a job we hate just to pay the bills? Staying in an unhappy relationship because we think we can't do better? Being unhealthy and unhappy because we never took the time to realise our worth? Before we know it, our time would be up and we would feel cheated out of a good *life* and most likely wish we'd been more organised or saved enough money to actually do something worthwhile with our time. We only have one life and this is your time to get a clear plan in your mind and heart and create the life of your dreams. Don't wait until you have lived your life and wished you had done something worthwhile. Don't live a life of regret, live a life of passion. Now is your time. Decide what kind of life you want and go make it happen.

Imagining your life like booking a holiday will help you to decide what you really want and the more specific you are, the more likely you are to get what you want. You may not know what your purpose is yet but you will know who you want to become. Our core values which are our guiding principles from lesson #1 are part of who we are and they will not change in life, only evolve as we do. We may change our direction but human beings very rarely change their core values. It is who we are.

What does your dream life look like?

We have already talked about what you want from yourself, from your relationships, from your health, so now we need to understand what you want from life itself. What do you want to do in life and what do you want to achieve?

When I was very young, I was fixated on becoming a hairstylist and nothing anyone could have said would have changed my mind. I had a dream and achieved it but as I grew, I wanted to progress more and new thoughts and ideas came into play. I wanted to try modelling.

From the age of 16, I had been asked to model for people from time to time. It started in college at a fashion show. I then modelled for a local photographer followed by various charity fashion shows. As much as I thought I was unattractive, they seemed to want me and my friend to model at their events, for free of course, and we were flattered.

I always agreed because: I felt I was giving my time to charities; Because I was asked (I used to be a 'yes' girl and didn't like to say no to people in case I upset them); Because it was actually lots of fun; Because I love a challenge and don't like fear controlling me.

Every time I did it though, I was terrified and had sleepless nights leading up to the event because I worried that people would discover the fraud that I was and realise I wasn't attractive enough to model for them. Anyway, over the years I began to enjoy it and wondered if I could actually get paid to do it. I loved clothes and dressing up anyway, so I thought maybe I should try. I did some research and made some calls (Who knew of internet then?), sent off some of my modelling photos and consequently joined a model agency at aged 29. I just thought I'd give it a shot; I was almost 30 so I thought it's now or never. I had nothing to lose except my dignity perhaps. People had told me over the years that I should model so I thought why not? Maybe five-foot 4¾ inch averaged looking females are the up and coming thing? Who knows? LOL. So, I was on the books of this modelling agency thinking I was the bee's knees, secretly hoping that I wouldn't be called as I was terrified. But then I got a call for a job in Glasgow for the tourist board. I spent the morning being photographed dressed up as a traffic warden, giving a handsome man a parking ticket along with a kiss on the cheek. I went home a happy lady with around £150 in my pocket, a bounce in my step and a smile on my face. Not bad for a couple of hours work I thought, I can do this.

That was my first and last job doing any other paid modelling work because I quit pretty soon after. I discovered that the average model spends their time working in promotions. I was offered work in nightclubs promoting drinks but that just wasn't my cup of tea. I did do one whole day in promotions standing in the local supermarket promoting a new mop though. It was the single most tedious day that I have ever experienced in my entire life and I said to myself, "Never again! This is not for me!" The reality is that this was the work that an average 'model' does a lot of the time. They promote. Some love this kind of work but I hated it. I had only been focused on the glamorous side, and I didn't love it enough to endure the not-so-glam side. I was certainly not super model material and I came to accept that I was not, and never would be, a unicorn. I was however extremely grateful that I tried. I know for sure that when I am on my deathbed in the future I will not look back and wonder if I should have tried modelling.

The one thing that I refuse to do is to leave this earth with regret for the things I didn't do, when I knew I had to try. It turned out that I didn't want to be a model after all. I had followed other people's suggestions and I thought it was a good idea at the time and even though I wasn't Britain's next top model, I'm so glad I ticked it off my to-do list. If I hadn't tried, I would have always wondered. Now I have my one day of professional modelling career on my list of fun experiences instead of on a list of regrets.

Many years ago, I was asked what I wanted for my life and how I wanted to be remembered. What small phrase would I want to be etched on my gravestone in remembrance of me and my life? This was one of the hardest questions that I ever had to answer. To imagine my grave and to see what words were written about me when I am gone was really hard, but this was the most significant question that led me to living a fulfilling and joy-filled life. It changed everything. It gave me a destination for my life's meaning. It brought me to an understanding of who I really am.

It took me two days of deep contemplation and a lot of tears to come up with the following phrase:

"SHE PUT LOVE IN OUR HEARTS AND SMILES ON OUR FACES."

This one sentence was engrained in my heart and will stay there until I die and I will dedicate my life to earning it. I do not want to leave instructions for what has to be written, I want those that love me to write what is in their hearts, not mine. But having this end result as my reason for being helps me to stay on track and reminds me of why I am here. My desire in life is to fill hearts with love and to help others to feel more joy in their lives. My journey so far has had its ups and downs but everything good and bad is taking me in the right direction.

Once we know why we are here, and what our reason for being is, we can then find various paths to point us in the right direction. Some paths lead us to knowing what we *don't* want (like my modelling), some paths lead to lessons that teach us something (depression taught me empathy, among other things) but all the paths we choose will eventually lead to where we want to be, to who we aspire to be. Denzel Washington said, "Don't aspire to make a living, aspire to make a difference!" and if each of us live our lives in this manner, we can all live happy and fulfilling lives no matter what the world is doing. Our basic human needs include, love, connection and significance and if we strive to be the best we can be, and plant seeds of love in all areas of our lives, home, work and relationships, then we will reap love in all areas of our lives. It's not what we have that makes us great, it's what we *do* with what we have.

A Personal Mission Statement

What is a personal mission statement? It is a declaration of the deeper purpose of your life. Not what you want to do for a living but who you want to be and what you want to dedicate your life to. My personal mission statement also evolves and grows as I do but writing down the purpose of our lives and reviewing it often helps us to be true to ourselves and keeps us moving forward. Before I wrote my own mission statement, I used a poem that I read every day to remind me of who I am:

> As I live each day
> may I do my part
> to make one difference,
> to touch one heart
> and through each day
> may it be my goal
> to encourage one mind
> and inspire one soul
>
> – Unknown Author

Reading this back now still gives me chills up my spine as a reminder of my life's purpose. These beautiful words are still etched upon my soul. But we are all so individual and each of our mission statements have to be written by our own hand for us to connect to our reason for being. Once we know *why* we are here, we can then work on the '*how* '. Having a mission statement reminds us daily that we matter and that we have a part to play. It is enough to get us out of bed in the morning, enough to pick ourselves up when we fall, enough to know that we have love to share, enough to know that we have something to give, regardless of how it is received. We fill our hearts through giving love, not receiving it, and only we can give a part of ourselves, so ultimately only we can fill our hearts.

My good friend Joyce sadly lost her 22-year-old daughter Judith to suicide many years ago. I never knew Judith but Joyce kindly shared this poem with me that I have hanging on my office wall to remind me of my mission and to remind me of the pain that some beautiful souls suffer. I believe with all my heart that my work can help young people to know their worth and to help them to overcome this level of pain in their lives by learning to love who they are, realising their significance in life, to know they matter, and to create incredible lives.

Dreams Turn to Dust
By Judith Scott

I dream of life on a secluded Island
I dream of running barefoot over soft golden sand
I dream of living beneath the sea as a mermaid
I dream of being one with the wildest of animals.
And being able to fly freely like the eagle

I want to stand on top of a snowy peaked mountain,
I want to reach out and embrace a life with God
I want to float lifelessly through a cloud filled sky
I want to look out on the world and see peace
And I want to find myself belonging to a good and safe culture.

Sadly, I find that in reality, dreams are just dust,
Sadly, I find that Mermaids and peace do not exist
Sadly, I find even the freedom of an eagle will not last forever
Sadly, I find, even God and mountains cannot be reached without a struggle
But none of these stop me trying to rid myself of the harness that restricts my life.

Sadly, Judith felt there was only one way to escape her pain but I believe she was not aware of her hand in her own life. She did not know of her power and potential because it is not taught in school. Sadly, she did not have this book as a guide to use to help her to understand and use her power to create another reality for herself.

Judith's story truly breaks my heart but it fuels my mission further. Because I *can* make a difference to lives, it is my moral duty to do all I can to try. The work that I do is bigger than me, bigger than my fear of failure and I have to listen to my heart, follow my mission and overcome any doubts that pop into my mind of how it will be received. It's what we sow that is important, the work that we put in, and why we do what we do, the rest is in the hands of the universe. This very book could potentially save a life and improve the lives of millions but that can only happen if I have enough faith and courage to write it. This is my life's mission and I will strive continually to do all I can to help anyone in need. It is not what I do, it's who I am.

We can all dream, that is the easy part but it's what we do with our dreams and desires that matter. We can act on them or we can keep them as dreams but which will light up our souls? In order to know where to start, we need to know what we want.

The following questions will help you to understand what you want to dedicate your life to and know your life's mission.

1. If you knew you could not fail, what would you do with your life and why would you do it?

2. What did you want to be when you were little and why did you want to do that? What feeling did you think you would feel by doing this job?

3. If you could learn one skill and be a master of it, what would it be?

4. What would you do with this new skill and why?

5. If you could spend your days doing what you love that could make a difference in the lives of others too, what would you do?

6. Close your eyes and take a few minutes to imagine yourself five or ten years from now. You are living the life of your dreams earning the money you want to earn and living happily.

a. Describe a perfect working day in your dream life in detail from the minute you wake until the minute you go to bed.

b. Describe in detail what a perfect free day would look like, doing what you love with who you love.

7. What are you passionate about, what could you talk for hours about and never get bored with? Explain in detail.

8. If you were obligated to write a book about your accomplishments, achievements or character in your life so far, to help others, what would your book be about?

9. If you could have the life of any other human being past or present, who's life would you want and why?

10. What does living a successful life look like in your mind?

11. Who do you know that is living a successful life right now and what makes them successful in your eyes?

12. If you had unlimited influence in this world and could change whatever you wanted about it to make it better, what three things would you change and why?

For example. I would introduce more life lessons, and mindset into the school curriculum so that children and teenagers realise that they can have any good thing in their lives if they understand and use their personal power.

a.

b.

c.

13. Imagine that you have reached the end of a happy and purpose-filled life and as you approach the pearly gates of heaven to meet God you contemplate all that you have done with the gifts, talents and passions that you were given. An angel asks you what good have you done with your life. What do you say?

(For example, I would say I gave life my all. I did my best to lift others up and to guide people to a happier life and a more loving heart. I didn't waste any of the gifts and talents I was given, I developed them and used them to the best of my ability. I opened my heart to everyone and I was there with open arms for anyone that needed me. I have loved and lived a happy life. I have left a legacy for others to learn from.)

What do you say to the angel?

The purpose of my life is to write, teach, coach and speak to the people of the world and if nobody wants to read, learn, take action or listen, that does not change my purpose. We do not need the world's recognition for our purpose, it is what we *give* that matters, not how it is received. All the greatest personalities in history were told they were not good enough, intelligent enough, talented enough, beautiful enough at some point in their lives but if they listened to the world, they would not be the heroes of our time.

– Albert Einstein's first teachers questioned whether he was intellectually disabled because of his inability to speak clearly. He hated school and was expelled from high school because of his attitude and behaviour. He also failed the entrance exam for university. Even though he excelled in maths and physics, he was under average for other subjects, but that didn't stop him from getting a place and becoming one of the world's greatest scientists. He not only impacted the world of science but the world in general, and his words are still inspiring people every day, more than 60 years after his death. One of my favourite quotes of his is: "A true sign of intelligence is not knowledge but imagination."

– Sir Richard Branson the international business mogul and founder of the Virgin label, is dyslexic and struggled academically when he was a child and said of himself: "I was seen as the dumbest person in school." His headmaster told him when he left school at 16 that he would either end up in prison or become a millionaire, but he didn't just become a millionaire, he became a billionaire. He received his knighthood in March 2000 for his 'services to entrepreneurship' and continues to inspire millions of people around the globe through his work and his books.

– Sylvester Stallone, titled as "one of the greatest action heroes of all time", was turned down for hundreds of acting jobs as nobody would hire him due to his slurred speech and odd-looking face. There had been difficulties during his birth which left him paralysed down the left side of his face. He moved to New York in pursuit of his dreams of becoming a movie star but after being rejected time and time again and having no money, he decided to write his own screenplay 'Rocky' with himself as the starring role. Again, his work was rejected but he never gave up, and finally someone agreed to produce the film with him starring as Rocky Balboa. The film grossed over $200 million in 1976 and went on to win three Oscars. Rocky not only spawned six sequels, but it has also been considered one of the greatest sports films ever made. Imagine if Sylvester Stallone had believed what others said about him? His determination and belief in his work made movie history.

What fuelled their determination to succeed? I believe it was love.

Creating a dream life and a dream job means falling in love with what we do and our life's mission. Doing so will sustain us in hard times when things don't go as planned. We adapt, change tactics, take another route but when we have love in our hearts and a clear destination, we will get there.

When a parent has a child, they never give up no matter how hard parenting gets. They power through the frustration and sleepless nights with their babies to do their very best, and give them their best. When their toddler has tantrums day in and day out, they never give up on their mission to teach, shape and nurture them. When their teenager is going through hormonal changes and turn into an irrational monster, they keep going, keep loving and keep working at their job being a good parent. Why? Because of pure love.

When our intentions are pure and we pour our heart and soul into what we do, we will never give up on what we believe in.

When we fall in love with our life's mission and have a dream, a clear vision and purpose, we power through rejection, ridicule and disappointment and keep moving forward. Failure does not become an option. If we don't achieve our dreams and aspirations it's not due to failure, it's due to quitting on ourselves. Who cares if nobody understands us or shares our vision? Who cares if they cannot see life from our perspective? If we know why we have such dreams and aspirations and continue to strive at living life with love in our hearts, then we cannot fail. We can fall, but we can also choose to pick ourselves up and keep moving. Our passion, dedication and love is enough to fuel our work in fulfilling our life's mission, whatever we choose to do.

What *do* I want to do with my life?

This is the question that people continually ask themselves but when they come up blank, they drop the question and keep dragging themselves through life hoping that one day they will find it. I know a lot of people in their fifties and sixties that still don't know what they want from life and have spent their whole lives hoping life will get better. Hope is wonderful but we cannot go through life hoping, we have to go through life actively doing things to make life better. I hear people say:

- If only I could meet 'The One', I would be happy.
- When I find a job that I love, I'll be happy.
- If I could earn good money, I'd be happy.
- When I retire, I'll be happy
- If only I could lose weight, I would be happy.

But guess what? Happiness never comes because they are waiting for it to appear, for the right time to start, for the answers to miraculously pop into their hearts and minds. The reality is that we need to actively seek to find what we are looking for. Imagine going on a treasure hunt but have no idea what the treasure actually is. Are we looking for gold, silver or precious stones? Are we looking for jewellery or money? Are we looking for ancient texts or artefacts? If we don't know what we are looking for, how are we supposed to find it? How will we know when we find it? Well how are we supposed to find the perfect work for us if we don't know what we are looking for? The journey of a thousand miles begins with a single step and so does understanding our purpose. Writing out our personal mission statement is a good place to start.

As I said before, we first need to understand how we want to feel, what we want to achieve in life and then we have to decide what we want to do. My mission statement says nothing about my work but everything about what I want to achieve in life, my purpose. When our work aligns with our mission and passion, we go through each day happily working instead of looking at the clock wondering when the day is going to end. Happiness isn't some future event or accomplishment. It is here, now, in every step forward in the right direction. I love the quote "If you do what you love, you never have to work a day in your life" and this is 100% true.

I am intolerant to a lot of things: cow dairy products, refined sugars, red meat, negative people, and work that I don't love. I am not kidding. I will not tolerate living a life where I don't love what I do. Yes, I have to do jobs that I don't like, like cleaning the toilet and weeding the garden, that is part of life but I downright refuse to spend hours and hours a day disliking what I do for a living. Life is too short to spend it doing things that don't bring us joy and lift us. We all have to do jobs we hate at times but in doing so we learn what we don't like and how we don't want to feel.

I learned at age 14 that I didn't want to work in a kitchen after spending three nights a week washing pots and pans in a local hotel. I learned that I didn't want to work in promotions after my day promoting a new mop in the supermarket. I learned that I didn't like retailing products that were not 100% in alignment with my values in my network marketing business but each of these experiences taught me something valuable about myself and pointed me in the direction that I needed to go which I am grateful for.

So how do you want to feel about your life's work and mission? There are so

160

many areas to work in and so many jobs so how do we choose? Again, we have to refer back to our guiding principles in love lesson #1 and use them to decide what is best for us. For example, one of my guiding principles is to feed myself and others only healthful foods so I could not work in a sweet shop. I also could not sell or promote alcohol or cigarettes for the same reasons. It would be like a vegetarian working as a butcher. What we need to do is decide what is important to us. What lights us up, what brings joy to our souls. I started my network marketing business because I thought it was exactly what I needed. I could work from home, retail products online and give people advice on supplements and natural skin products but some of the products were not 100% natural and I could not promote them. If I wouldn't use them myself how could I ask others to?

I remember hearing a story about a woman and her little boy standing in line for hours to speak to Gandhi because she wanted him to help her son to stop eating sweets as they are bad for his health. After waiting two hours she finally came face to face with Gandhi and explained why she had come to see him. He said, "I can't help you now but come back in two weeks." The lady left a little annoyed that she had waited for two hours and he said nothing. But two weeks later, when she stood before him again after waiting in line, he put his hand on the little boy's head and said, "Don't eat sweets because they are bad for you!" The woman just looked at Gandhi as if to say, "That's it? That is all you are going to say?" and he turned and said, "I couldn't ask anyone to do something that I wasn't doing myself so since I saw you last; I have given up sweets."

I love this story and love Gandhi's philosophy. If we all go through life living in alignment with our guiding principles in our personal and professional life, we can live in peace knowing that we are doing what is right in our hearts. Doing what I do now, is in full alignment with my values, and with my life's mission and I have never been happier.

I believe there are two types of people. Some are more intellectual and some are more intuitive but neither are better than the other. We all have degrees of both but we usually lean to, and make decisions based on which side we feel more connected to. There is a need for both types of people but when we realise who we are, we will find it easier to decide what our true purpose is in life. Trouble comes when we try to be who we are not, and we tend to do that a lot. We often try to be who we think we ought to be or who others expect us to be, instead of who we truly are. My mantra for life is "KNOW MYSELF; LOVE MYSELF; BE MYSELF" because we can only be at peace with ourselves if we are being ourselves. Let me explain.

Just because someone is intelligent and can be a lawyer doesn't mean that they should be. If they want to be a lawyer because they are passionate about law and justice, then they should become a lawyer. If they are doing it because they were encouraged to do it by their parents, tutors or friends even if they had no passion for law, or they do it for the money or label to make them feel significant, then they are not living in alignment with who they are and they will not feel at peace.

When I had my hair salon, I had a client that was a lawyer and we talked a lot about life and I gave him a copy of a book I had read 'The Secrets of Abundant Happiness' by Adam J Jackson (my first self-development book that made me fall in love with self-development). We both talked about how we felt trapped and unhappy in our work and felt stuck. We talked about living our dream lives and consequently I sold up and moved abroad and soon after he sold his law firm and started working doing manual labour and working on his music. Thankfully his wife was really supportive of his decision and he was so much happier.

Obviously, people thought he was crazy, but why live a life that doesn't feel right or make us feel good about who we are, no matter how successful we are or how much money we make? We can choose to fill our souls with what we love or fill our pockets with money, but if we work smart *and* hard, we can fill both doing what we love and living our passion. If we make choices to please others, we will ultimately be unhappy.

When Gary, one of my trainee hairdressers started working with us at 16, he struggled in hairdressing. I had to put extra hours in to get him through his training because it just wasn't coming naturally to him. He saw hairdressing as a good business and thought it would be a good way to earn a good living as he could see how successful our business was. We laughed about it after because at 16 he thought that we kept all the money that we tilled. He hadn't considered, rent, products, wages, energy bills, taxes etc. It was obvious that his heart was not in hairdressing but he didn't know what else to do. He didn't love hairdressing but we had so much fun at work that it didn't feel like work. We were a great team of people and spent our days laughing and chatting to our clients and just happened to be doing their hair at the same time. I remember asking Gary what he loves and what his passion was and he said History and English. I was totally shocked at his answer as he didn't look like the academic type but he said that the only job he could really do with history and English was to be a teacher, so at 16 settled for learning a trade and hairdressing seemed easy enough. Gary and I got on like a house on fire but not due to what we had in common. I hated history, to me it was the most boring subject on the planet yet this strapping young man covered in tattoos was fascinated with it. He was in fact a nerd at heart and settled for hairdressing but soon after I sold up, he left too and tried his hand at other things. Barber and tattoo artist among other things but eventually he listened to his heart and went on to university to study History and English. Almost 20 years on, he is now happily working as a college lecturer, living in alignment with his heart and in his element as he spends his days talking about his favourite subjects, shares his passion and knowledge and gets to call it work.

When we do what we love our hearts are fuelled with energy and passion that radiates good to the world and good into our own souls.

My life's mission statement:

The purpose of my life is to be a beacon of love and light in the world, to inspire those that walk this life with me and to teach and guide them to live happy, healthy and purposeful lives.

This is my personal mission statement and now it is time for you to write yours.

Your mission statement

The purpose of my life is to…

What Are Life's Riches?

I think the majority of young people dream about becoming rich and famous, but why? I know when I was young, I certainly thought money and fame would give me what I wanted in life. Unlimited funds to buy what I want and to afford to travel the world if I choose. To feel significant for my work and feel valued. To be loved and adored by millions. To live an exciting life rubbing shoulders with other rich and famous people. To live a varied and luxury lifestyle, being able to choose what I want to do all day. To gain the freedom and control over my time.

But is that reality? Do we have to be rich and famous to feel so wonderful? Do the rich and famous love their lives that much? If so, why do so many of them turn to drugs and alcohol? Why do so many take their own lives if they have everything they could ever want and need? Perhaps it's not as it seems. I would not know because I have never been there but when I see some of Hollywood's stars, I wonder how they actually *feel* about their lives.

I know that I am a person that is happy with my life and happy living a simple life. I have the freedom to be me, to go where I want, when I want, to do what I want when I want. I am free to spend my days how I choose and I am neither rich nor famous, but I am happy.

To me life's riches are not all fame and fortune, they are:

- TIME
- LOVING RELATIONSHIPS
- FAMILY
- FREEDOM
- GOOD HEALTH
- HIGH ENERGY
- HAPPINESS
- KINDNESS
- CONNECTION
- FRIENDSHIP
- PURPOSEFUL LIVING
- FAITH AND SPIRITUAL CONNECTION
- PASSION
- PROSPERITY
- WISDOM
- LONGEVITY

- PEACE
- HARMONY
- BALANCE

There was once a good and kind young man called Gennaro that owned a piece of land in the beautiful Tuscan hills in Italy. On this land, there were vines that produced the most delicious grapes which he made into delicious wine that he sold to make a good living. Gennaro fell in love, got married and had a family, and he and his wife lived a wonderfully simple life working on the land, producing wine and by running a small authentic Tuscan bed and breakfast from the barn which they converted into rooms. They loved their life, spent their days working on the land, and spent their evenings as a family socialising with guests eating outside overlooking the beautiful view and watching the sunset behind the curves of the hills.

On one occasion an American businessman came to visit and experience the Tuscan life and stayed a few days. He fell in love with the area and with the family. One evening, the two men sat after dinner sipping their delicious wine chatting, admiring the stunning backdrop and the businessman started to offer some business advice to Gennaro about how he could up level his life and income in the future by investing some money into his business. Gennaro was happy to listen as the businessman talked with such passion and excitement. He talked about how he could turn his land into a retreat for those that needed a complete rest away from the busyness of the world. To build some chalets, a swimming pool and spa and employ some staff to make an exclusive and beautiful retreat and resort. Gennaro let the businessman finish talking and then asked: "But why would I do that?"

The businessman said, "So that after 10–15 years of hard work you will be able to retire and hire people to run the business for you and you can spend your days however you choose enjoying life with your family doing what you love most." The businessman said, "Imagine how wonderful your life would be?"

"I don't need to imagine it," replied Gennaro "I'm already living it!" The businessman laughed out loud nodding his head in concurrence.

Each of us have our own version of what our dream life looks like and feels like to us, and if we truly know what is important to us, and what life's treasures are to us, we can each live our dream lives. We often get sucked into other people's thoughts, ways of thinking, and ideas of what a dream life *should* look like but when we listen to our own hearts and minds and follow our own direction, we will succeed in reaping life's treasures.

What are your top ten life's riches that you aspire to gain in your life, i.e. Happiness, wealth, health, peace, purpose, loving relationships, marriage, parenthood, etc.

1.
2.
3.
4.
5.
6.
7.

8.
9.
10.

Discipline and Consistency

No matter what we desire in life, we do not get it given to us, and we don't just do something once to achieve our goals, it is down to creating new habits and rituals that we have to work on consistently every day.

If we need to lose weight, we can't diet for weeks and months, get to our ideal weight and expect our weight to stay off. We need to make these changes part of who we are forever, to achieve and maintain the standard of life we want. Those that diet constantly and restrict their calories or eat no carbohydrates can certainly lose weight but as soon as they go back to eating normally, the weight piles back on and usually plus some, as the person's metabolism has been messed up and becomes much slower. The body's organs have suffered from insufficient nutrients and their health can be compromised. With 'yo-yo' dieting comes 'yo-yo' health and 'yo-yo' self-esteem levels. Creating good habits by making good meal choices, consuming sufficient nutrients, exercising and working on maintaining a good mindset means we can maintain a new and achievable lifestyle that can sustain us.

The same goes for all areas of life. We need to create good working habits and work consistently on our goals and dreams to achieve them. We have to keep moving and growing in order to feel truly fulfilled in life.

If we are striving only to make money, we can find ways, maybe not legal or sustainable ways but we can always find a way. Like dieting, if we don't commit to changing our lifestyle, our cash flow will yo-yo as well as our peace of mind and self-worth.

In the business world, we hear of people making lots of money but also losing it just as quickly as they made it, usually leaving behind debt. We hear of everyday people winning millions in the lottery and losing it all in a few months because they did not spend it wisely. Well, we have to think of life in that way too. If we waste our talents, we lose them. If we waste our money, we will lose it; if we mistreat our bodies, we will lose our good health. If we waste our time, we will lose it... We can never earn back time that we have lost so let's make our lives count.

Once we know what we want, make a plan, work on our plan consistently regardless of the outcome, we will get results. There is no such thing as failure.

Only winning or learning.

Everything I have ever achieved in my life I put down to discipline and consistency. When I started my first business as a salon owner, I showed up every day consistently with high standards of excellence. When I turned my health around, I created new lifestyle habits and stuck to them consistently. When I decided to start running, I set myself weekly goals and never strayed. Even when I decided to write my first book, I made a goal of writing at least one page every single day, no matter what. When I wrote each day, I marked a big red cross on my desk calendar and I made a commitment to myself to never miss a day. Some days it would be late at night but I refused to go to bed until I saw that big red cross marked off. This was progress and every single day took me a step closer to achieving my goal.

Growth Mindset

Having a growth mindset means that whatever you want in life you can have because you will adapt, grow and learn what you need, to get what you want, and be who you want. It's an understanding that everything we want to achieve in our lives is like working on building muscles in our body. It takes daily practise and action to grow, but also continual work to maintain and sustain them.

Those with a growth mindset also try to see what they can learn from life's difficult lessons instead of allowing them to weigh them down and take them out of the game. So instead of asking "Why did this have to happen?" they ask "What did I need to learn from this and how can I use this to become better?" The opposite of having a growth mindset is having a fixed mindset. Meaning that we put limits on what we think we can achieve and do. I like to think of myself as having a growth mindset but the reality is that we have to keep building that muscle too and if we don't use it, we lose it. For a time, I had a fixed mindset and that was the reason that I didn't speak Italian for so many years. I told myself that I was not good at speaking Italian because it didn't come easily to me but the truth was that if I wanted to speak Italian, I would have put the work in to learn. I used to get upset and hate myself for not being good enough or clever enough to learn but the problem was not my intelligence but my fixed mindset and my unwillingness to improve.

Another example of this was when I was living my dream life as a mummy to my two babies. I was so engrossed in them and loving motherhood that I shut out the world. I didn't have any interest in progressing in the world of technology, in fact, I hated computers and all technology because I didn't understand them (I left school in 1985 and we didn't have computers in school then)

So, as my kids grew, I realised that I had been left behind. I thought that I didn't need technology (fixed mindset), that I could go through life without it, but the reality was that if I wanted to get my life back, I had to learn, grow and develop myself to update my brain and my mind. I couldn't possibly do all I wanted to do without updating my life so I had to step out of my comfort zone, step into the unknown and into the scary world of technology. I had to teach myself how to use a PC and learn how to type. I started with one finger and worked my way up. Since then I have typed hundreds of thousands of words while writing my books but if I had held on to my fixed mindset, my books would still be a dream. Dreams will remain dreams until we make them reality.

If we have a fixed mindset it is most likely because of the labels we put on ourselves, or our parents and others put on us. I was guilty of this myself as a parent. I remember telling my son when he was practising a song for a school concert that he inherited his monotone singing voice from his Granny. He already believed that he was a bad singer and I confirmed his beliefs by telling him that. He'd decided that because his Granny was the same, then he could do nothing to change the outcome.

It's one thing to be told that you inherited a family member's eyes but it's quite another to have inherited their negative attributes. My mum could not sing well. She did sing only one note and so did my son, but they had never been taught. All it took was for me to teach my little boy *how* to change his tone when singing. I know this sounds too simple but it worked. I spent an hour with him showing him how and he began singing well and he felt so much better about himself. My mum spent her whole life singing in monotone (unfortunately for us), not because she was a bad singer but because she never tried to learn how to sing well.

When we hear ourselves saying "I can't…", we have to ask ourselves whether it is actually true or whether we are living with a fixed mindset and making excuses for not being better, instead of working on being better. We have to be aware of the labels we are carrying and whether they are holding us back or allowing us to live abundantly. Instead of saying "I can't," we have to change it to "I can't…*yet!*"

People with a growth mindset are happier, persist more, like challenges, grow intellectually, are always looking to improve and be better. Because of this, they become more successful at anything they do. They adapt, change, learn and improve in order to succeed in all areas of life and are happy growing. Those with a fixed mindset are restricted in their endeavours as they believe there is no room for improvement, that this is as good as it gets, that life cannot be changed and they accept less than they desire in life. Most people have a fixed mindset and believe that what they know to be true is true and that they are right, but when we open our minds and allow them to grow, absolutely anything is possible. Adopting a growth mindset will help us to see a world of endless opportunities, endless growth, endless happiness and fulfilment and bring excitement and energy into our lives. Again, we get to choose.

Hundreds of years ago in China during the Song dynasty it became a custom to bind little girl's feet because having tiny feet was a sign of beauty. From as young as four or five years old, they would have their feet bound really tightly with strips of cloth to stop their feet from growing so they had to suffer excruciating pain. Because their feet were bound and didn't grow, these poor girls lost their ability to walk with ease and their well-being was compromised, all to look good in society.

We may not bind our feet these days but some of us still bind ourselves with self-doubt and fear that restricts our personal growth and stops us from moving freely, being our true selves. Our bonds are invisible but we can still suffer the pain of being trapped in a life that we feel we have no power over. Once we break the bonds of a fixed mindset and rid ourselves of self-doubt and fear, we are free to be and do any good thing that our heart desires.

Comfort Zones or Lazy Bones?

There are so many reasons why people don't reach their true potential and live their lives fully, but who is to say that they have to? When I was a full-time mummy, I couldn't have been happier. I love the simple things in life, sun, sea, picnics on the beach, walks in nature, being with my family, cuddled up on the couch watching a movie with my kids…the list goes on and on. I don't feel a need to be famous or well-known but I do feel a need to share my experience in life for others to learn from. My intention for my life is to be a hand for others to hold so they know they are never alone. This is what makes me feel whole but in order to do that, I needed to step out of my comfort zone and get uncomfortable in order to be able to live my purpose.

One of the main reasons why some people don't go for what they want in life is fear of stepping out of their comfort zones. I like to think of our comfort zones as being like living in our own little egg.

Inside our shell we feel safe and protected and hidden from the world but if we do not ever leave that egg, we will never see the light of day and never experience the true beauty of life. We have no idea of the treasures that are ahead and we barely live at all. Yes, it is safe but safe from what? Being in, and staying in, our shells is like putting ourselves into prison where we only dream of freedom.

Some people grow a little and make a crack in their shell to let a little light in, look out but still stay well-hidden and protected. They only hope and dream that one day they will experience life and its treasures but stay where they are safely tucked away. They fear the unknown and wish they were brave enough to break out but remain a spectator and ask themselves why life is so unfair.

Some crack through and open up their shell, they learn and grow and are inspired by those that are living the dream but again due to fear and self-doubt, they stay where they are trying to build up the courage to overcome their fear and leave the safety of their shell but never quite make it. I believe this is where the majority of people stay. They are not unhappy but they also want so much more. They make attempts at leaving their shell but never quite manage to break free. They have big hopes and dreams of a better future and a better world but their doubts stop them as they fear failure.

Others grow so much that their shell becomes a restriction, they no longer fit into the tiny space and they automatically breakthrough and crack open their shell. Living there does not become an option because they have outgrown that space. They see the true beauty of the world and are grateful for the gift of life. They spread their wings and see the world and all its beauty from the sky, high in the clouds. They are free to go and experience all of life with a spectacular view. This is the true beauty of life.

These people want to help their brothers and sisters that are still in their shells but know they cannot break them free because the shell can only be broken from the inside and those within the shell have to want to fly.

We choose our lives. We can choose a simple life or a lifetime adventure and it is not obligatory to fly and experience the world from an aerial view but to be happy in life we have to make progress and grow. Your dream life could be sailing around the world on your private luxury yacht, but it could just as easily be living in a one-bed cottage in the Scottish Highlands with your dog. I can't tell you what your dream life looks like, but what is important is that it is your dream and your dream alone.

1. At what stage are you in your growth level within your own shell? Explain how you feel.

2. What stage do you want to reach in your life and why?

3. Do you have a fixed mindset or growth mindset? If you want to live your dream life what has to change within yourself?

My Life's Achievements

Imagine yourself in the far and distant future sitting on a swing chair in an idyllic setting, looking out at the beautiful sunset. You have a big smile on your face as you review your life with gratitude, the dream life that you created, doing everything that you wanted to do. You have lived your life to the fullest and have no regrets...

What are your greatest achievements?
For example:

I wrote multiple international bestselling books.
I have been extremely happily married for many years.
I have helped millions of people to be happier through understanding their personal power and by creating themselves abundant lives

1.

2.

3.

4.

5.

6.

Mindset Reminders

- Know yourself.
- Love yourself.
- Be yourself.
- Be your own best friend.
- Focus on, and look for the good things in life. We always find what we are looking for.
- Live according to your own guiding principles.
- The secret to living is giving.
- Take responsibility for your own life.
- You are 'The One' that will complete you.
- Remember that perfection does not exist.
- Plant good seeds because we reap what we sow.
- Treat others as you want to be treated.
- Do everything with love and kindness.
- Build your self-worth by serving others.
- Remember that only hurt people, hurt people.
- Forgive always, the only person it hurts is you.
- Remove the stones that are weighing you down and stopping you from moving forward.
- Let go of things that don't serve you, the past, negativity, blame etc.
- Remember that we are all equal no matter who we are or what we do.
- Be grateful for all things, good and bad. All things shape us into who we are meant to be.
- You cannot fail, you can only learn lessons or quit.
- Be the kind of person you want to see in the world.
- Good health is true wealth.
- Your body is a gift, treat it with love and respect.
- Develop your gifts and talents.
- Create good daily habits that serve you.
- Every journey begins with a single step.
- Be consistent and never give up on yourself.
- It's not what you have that matters, it's what you do with what you have that counts.
- No one can make you happy, or unhappy, it's all up to you.
- Ask and it shall be given.
- Adopt a growth mindset.
- Step out of your comfort zone, it's where you can truly be free to live.
- You are the creator of your own destiny.
- Think kind thoughts and you will always look lovely.
- Don't compare yourself with others, only with the best version of you.

- Believe in yourself.
- Live your purpose…we all have something unique to give.
- Love always, and be the best that you can be.

Conclusion

Before us lies two paths – honesty and dishonesty.
The short-sighted embark on the dishonest path;
the wise on the honest.
For the wise know the truth;
in helping others, we help ourselves;
and in hurting others we hurt ourselves.
Character over shadows money,
and trust rises above fame.
Honesty is still the best policy.

– Napoleon Hill

The most important work we will ever do in our lives is on ourselves, being the best that we can be in order to share the best of who we are. The purpose of life is not to achieve greatness in the eyes of the world but to grow the love in our hearts to share with the world.

If we have been blessed with love and strength we were born to support, love and strengthen those in need.

If we have been blessed with wisdom and knowledge, we were born to awaken the world to wisdom and knowledge.

If we have been blessed with a desire to heal and save lives, we are here to learn and grow in order to heal and save lives.

If we have been blessed with great faith and understanding we are here to lift and teach faith and the ways of God.

It is our moral obligation to spend our lives in the service of others. To share our gifts to lift up those that are in need and to be a light in a world of ever-increasing darkness, for them to find their way. Following the good in our hearts will lead us to all good things and this is where we will receive the greatest rewards. I can promise you that this is a path of happiness and where we find life's true treasures…

Now you have the rules of the game… Go and win yourself a gold medal in this game of life… It is your birth right.

Wishing you all abundant happiness, health and love in your lives, and peace and harmony in your ever-growing hearts.

With much love always,
Nadia xxx